Art and the Handicapped Child

Art and the handicapped child

Zaidee Lindsay

 VAN NOSTRAND REINHOLD COMPANY New York

Studio Vista London

Author's note

The terms E.S.N. (Educable subnormal) and S.S.N. (Severely subnormal) are used in Britain for children with I.Q.s assessed at between 50 and 75, and 30 and 55 respectively. The American equivalent terms are 'Educable mentally retarded' and 'Trainable mentally retarded.'

Van Nostrand Reinhold Company Regional Offices:
New York   Cincinnati   Chicago   Millbrae   Dallas

Van Nostrand Reinhold Company International Offices:
London   Toronto   Melbourne

Copyright © 1972 by Zaidee Lindsay
Library of Congress Catalog Card Number 74-180235
ISBN 0-442-24799-0

Printed in the U.S.A.
First published in England by Studio Vista Ltd.
35, Red Lion Square, London, WC1R 4SG
Published in the U.S.A. in 1972 by Van Nostrand Reinhold Company
A Division of Litton Educational Publishing, Inc.
450 West 33rd Street, New York, N.Y. 10001

16   15   14   13   12   11   10   9   8   7   6   5   4   3   2

Contents

Preface

Although I have no medical or teaching experience with handicapped children, I have had opportunities to see many examples of their work, and the general impression I have gained is that it compares very favourably with that of children who are not physically or mentally handicapped.

It is not perhaps surprising that children with severe physical handicaps often achieve the most positive and intense results, for we all know that the will to overcome gives added strength to purpose.

What may be more difficult to explain are the simple, direct and often beautiful designs produced by those who are described as educationally sub-normal, which sometimes makes one wonder whether the initials E.S.N. are a true or complete indication of mental capacity, for although this may not be normal, in some respects it may not necessarily be sub-normal, and encouragement in self-expression through the Arts could well lead to greater confidence and mental well-being, and in the case of the autistic child, the Arts may be the only way that thoughts can find expression.

Certainly the autistic and some of the educationally sub-normal children do not seem lacking in sensibility, which makes one feel that perhaps more consideration of the relationship between sense and sensibility might lead to enlightening conclusions which would be valuable both to the children and to those who so nobly work for them. This book points the way to these conclusions, and I wish it all success.

W. T. Monnington, P.R.A.
29.9.71.

Preface to the American Edition

Out of a rich and warm experience with 'special' pupils has developed this needed book on physically handicapped children and the creative art incentives developed for them by an English teacher. Although Zaidee Lindsay never uses first person terminology, her love and concern for handicapped youngsters shines through her explanations and descriptions.

Little abstract theory is offered in *Art and the Handicapped Child*; rather, the approach maintained throughout is simply: 'This is how things are.' Teachers already working in the difficult Special Education field as well as art therapists in clinic and hospital settings will find the book especially rich in new ideas and suggestions, and much of value can be gleaned by the teacher of slow normal pupils. The college instructor, vexed by inability to find an appropriate text for a first course in art for handicapped children will find the solution to his problem here.

As Miss Lindsay points out, 'creative' activities for physically and mentally handicapped children may seem a misnomer at first glance, but in America, at least, we are too prone to peg 'creativity' only at those high levels which have emerged from our vast literature on the subject since World War II, and especially since Sputnik, when the pursuit of 'creativity' and its applications became almost a national fetish. Miss Lindsay shows that there are creative levels which can be striven for realistically by even the most handicapped child when an innovative teacher leads him into exploration of the upper levels of his potentiality – an approach much needed in those American art classes in which pupils are, by definition, assumed to be incapable of any creative action.

Thus, the rationale of this book is much in line with a rising American trend – that children learn best, not through cold insistence on academics, but through the emotional and effective subjects. Our recent experiences with disadvantaged children have demonstrated the necessity for enrichment through the seeing, hearing, feeling, and moving modes of expression. When academic learning follows after, rather than precedes, the warm glow that comes through success and consequent self-image enhancement in artistic (or musical, dance, or dramatic) achievements, the chance for greater academic achievement is enlarged. Miss Lindsay's whole approach offers implications worthy of investigation by directors of learning for 'normal' children.

In *Art and the Handicapped Child* variations in terminology between the English and American systems of education occur but are understandable within the context in which they are used. Americans are accustomed to the fourfold classification recommended by the President's Panel on Mental Retardation of 1962. The first two divisions, Mild (IQ 50-70) and Moderate (IQ 35-49), apparently correspond to the English E.S.N. – educationally subnormal; and the American third and fourth divisions, Severe (IQ 20-34) and Profound (IQ below 20), seem to correspond to the English S.S.N. – severely subnormal. American classification is more likely to group physical handicaps together, with psychotic children handled in separate classifications. In *Art and the Handicapped Child* physical and emotional handicapping is not differentiated, although emotional interferences are pointed out. In America, the autistic child is recognized as psychotic and causes for his actions are sought in psychological dynamics which may dictate approaches to his recovery.

An especially impressive feature of the book are the descriptions of behaviour patterns of actual children – a feature which makes the book 'come alive'.

Art and the Handicapped Child is a welcome and much needed addition to the growing literature on creative art for exceptional children.

Dr Mary Lee Hodnett
Associate Professor of Art
Chairman for Art Education
The University of Texas at Arlington
Arlington, Texas

Introduction

Art education – for what purpose?

This book is intended primarily for those who are involved in the field of special education, but will interest all teachers with 'difficult' or slow-learning pupils in their class, student teachers and parents. This is because in attempting to find suitable creative activity for the handicapped child, one inevitably becomes concerned with fundamental learning processes.

A book which includes creative activities for both the physically and mentally handicapped child may not at first seem feasible to even the most casual observer, who will have realized the diverse nature of the many handicaps which can afflict the human race. Investigation will also show the subject to be further complicated because handicaps do not necessarily occur singly so that, in fact, the handicapped child may suffer multiple handicapping. The teacher who is primarily concerned with how this affects the behaviour and ability of the pupil must learn to look beyond these outward signs to find the real clues, for however we may classify children according to their physical and mental handicaps, there will often be no well-defined categories even within any one group. Nevertheless, the varied handicaps described in this book indicate from a practical educational view one recurring factor throughout, which is that most of these children are unable to respond normally to outside stimuli. Careful observation of a handicapped child during creative activity will often reveal how any acquirement of new experiences can be delayed, distorted or even made impossible by his handicaps. I have tried, therefore, to select the main stumbling blocks to creativity and give a practical as well as a theoretical approach to this whole subject. I have not linked individual handicaps with specific activities as the high incidence of multiple handicapping would make this impracticable. It is left to the reader to select the activities best suited to each individual child.

Art education for the handicapped child may be so directed that it becomes the means of inducing some response by increasing physical awareness in each situation, without which little educational or social development is possible. Creative activity can then be used for developing manual dexterity and patterns of movement; it encourages social communicability; it is psychotherapeutic in helping to restore confidence; it helps the child to master his environment through control of tools and materials; it encourages observation, discrimination of colour, shape and texture and stimulates imagination.

The term 'self-expression' has now been used in art education for a very long time and, as with most clichés, often without considering its full implication. Drawing, painting and modelling have become acceptable ways in which normal children can communicate ideas, although they do not necessarily show us how children actually see the world around them, and could be mainly an expression of experiences gained through senses other than sight, which children state according to their particular stage of development. One is familiar with the gap left between earth and sky which is a statement of experience not to be learned through visual stimulation alone.

Many handicaps definitely obstruct the normal movements and senses that are required for creativity and it might seem a contradiction to suggest that creative activities could play any useful part in helping to overcome such obstacles. This, however, merely draws our attention to another aspect of handicap. We are speaking of those who, because many if not all of the other activities have been denied them, have the greatest need of creative expression and yet often lack the basic means to express themselves even in this way. Creative activity can often provide the key to some solution of their problem.

Although provision of sensory experiences for very young children is now generally acceptable to most people, when once the child reaches junior school stage there does not seem to be the same appreciation of a need for such activity. Free expression can then so easily resolve into illustration or craftwork of a purely representational kind. Results are sometimes judged on whether they appear to achieve naturalistic representation, as this still remains for many adults the only criterion by which one can adequately assess creativity or even normal progress.

One of the main difficulties when teaching art to older pupils, including adults, is in developing their powers of observation and often this can only be achieved successfully through increasing their sensory awareness. It is even more important that those who are physically or mentally handicapped should be helped in this way as they are often limited in other forms of expression too, and so, unless given some positive outlet, will always remain inadequate. One can only appreciate fully how such experiences are acquired after working with those whose sensory mechanism has been affected in some way and for whom a visual approach to creativity is impracticable.

Some knowledge of handicaps and the ways in which many handicapped pupils may be helped to overcome or by-pass them will suggest art teaching methods not only for the physically and mentally handicapped, but could lead to a reappraisal of the role that art education could take in our ordinary schools.

Background

During this century a complete revolution in attitudes towards the handicapped has taken place, with the result that many today are receiving an education who formerly would have been classified as mentally defective and therefore quite incapable of learning. At a period when an academic approach was the only criterion in educational achievement, relative to which any other form of education could only be conceived as an adulterated version, it was conceded that some useful training might be given to these children. They were provided with what was considered to be suitable occupation, such as laundry work and boot repairing, for the merest suggestion then that any might express themselves creatively would have seemed ludicrous. In such an educational climate, society therefore approved the education system for the handicapped which was to become little more than 'occupational care'.

Although doctors had been aware of and had been treating cerebral palsy for several years before the Second World War, few children with this condition had been considered worth educating in any way. The autobiography of Dr Earl Carlson, an American, was published in 1941. It was particularly remarkable because he had been severely handicapped himself, but despite his physical disabilities had qualified as a doctor and become a specialist in the treatment of cerebral palsy. The interest which this aroused started a spate of research into the subject, and it was discovered that the incidence of cerebral palsy among children of school age was as much as one per thousand, and that over half of these had the same range of I.Q. as normal pupils in school. It was thus made apparent that some means of educating these children had to be found. Their plight soon stimulated public imagination and sympathy with the result that special schools or centres have continued to be established for 'spastics', as they became generally termed.

At the same time a basic change in the teaching methods for the partially sighted was taking place. It had previously been believed that what little sight they might have must be preserved and that therefore they should use it as little as possible. The partially sighted had actually been taught to write their names on a blackboard while standing with their backs to it, in order that eyes should be averted from the task. It also had been seriously believed that some permanent damage might be caused to the eyeballs by the forces of gravity if a partially-sighted person were allowed to look downwards. A teacher might therefore have found himself severely reprimanded had he allowed any members of his class to do so as they filed along. Once it was realized that no harm could be done by making the best use of any available sight, education for the partially-sighted pupil began to be developed in this direction.

During the past twenty years, the educational needs of physically handicapped pupils have altered considerably, owing to an actual change in the pattern of child handicap. Formerly, many of those attending special school had started life normally before developing skeletal tuberculosis or poliomyelitis which were then common. They therefore had some background comparable with that of normal healthy children upon which all future learning could be developed. Today the ranks of those with acquired handicaps are relatively small and usually include children who have been injured or others with muscular dystrophy.

A phenomenal drop in infant mortality during the years following the Second World War, coupled with increasing medical knowledge, meant that many more children with mental or physical defects were surviving. At the same time educational research, now focused upon the backward child, emphasized the development of methods in teaching generally that would be more attuned to the pupil's individual needs. The knowledge becoming available had caused a reappraisal of the various handicaps to be made and gradually there emerged other classified groups, not only because more accurate diagnosis was possible in some cases, but also owing to the presence of pupils who had survived with conditions which hitherto had proved fatal. The majority of special school places today are taken by children who have multiple handicaps. Not only are they handicapped from birth but the nature of their handicaps will often make it difficult for them to acquire even the most rudimentary knowledge, and this poses considerable educational problems.

Most of these children are now able to receive their education in schools and units established for a specific handicap or in ordinary schools, with home and hospital teaching also available. Their right to equality of educational opportunity and the need to provide different types of school was at last recognized in Britain by a recommendation in the 1944 Education Act that schools for the handicapped should be reorganized to follow the same pattern as the national system of education. The role of special schools for the mentally handicapped was also altered, since children who were considered ineducable or 'severely subnormal' (S.S.N.) had been removed to training centres, leaving those who were termed 'educationally subnormal' (E.S.N.) but capable of receiving some education. It is now realized that many S.S.N. children respond to educational methods which can be adapted to their needs. Since 1971 the British Education Act has been further implemented with the transfer of these centres from the local departments of public health to the education authorities.

Today there are not enough places available in special schools to accommodate more than ten per cent of those who are educationally subnormal, although some authorities provide special classes for dull and backward children and offer various kinds of remedial teaching. It would seem that there should be a fuller use of specific remedial creative experience for such pupils who remain at primary and secondary schools, where there are also others, even in a higher I.Q. range, with serious learning disabilities who might benefit from such activity.

The sentimental attitude which had grown up with the original system of provision for the handicapped was motivated by the principle that they should be kept in isolation from life and all its demands. This idea has often proved difficult to eradicate, although it only helps to preserve a negative approach to the whole subject of handicap. Gradually a more realistic attitude has emerged in which the main features of each handicap are studied so that attempts can be made to compensate for or at least to minimize its effects. It is then often possible to stretch the learning skills of these handicapped children.

Many local authorities in Britain have recently established diagnostic classes or assessment units so that children's progress can be evaluated with a view to recommending various types of educational treatment. The therapy of creative activities will inevitably play an important part in assessing progress and it is therefore necessary that we consider how these activities can be adapted to help those pupils within the different handicapped groups.

Visual handicaps

The major portion of what the normal child learns will be gained through sight and since most teaching is therefore based upon a visual approach, achievement comes to be linked closely with vision development and efficiency. Because those mechanisms which control all necessary eye movements, focus, and image fusion are functions of the brain, it will be realized that any dysfunction or disability in the central nervous system affecting these could not only seriously handicap a child in actual educational performance, but also influence his whole pattern of behaviour.

During the normal course of development, the very young child gradually learns to co-ordinate all ocular movement concerned with the focusing and convergence of both eyes. Only when this process has become fully integrated will it be possible for him to see any object singly and clearly. Visual performance will then continue to develop as he gradually learns to adjust this focus so that he can discriminate, make comparisons of shape or colour and work out spatial relationships from his surroundings.

Even the basic ocular gymnastics which we take almost for granted in our students will include their ability to see clearly, not only close to but at a distance, and to change fixation upwards and downwards or from side to side. Much of their learning depends upon the visual memory. It is therefore obvious from such cursory knowledge alone, that all these different aspects have to be considered in assessing visual competence.

Among children classified as blind, not all are entirely without sight, but many have restricted or variable vision. Although this will be insufficient for working by sight and braille will be used, it may still enable them to find their way about and to participate in activities that require the use of rather general vision only. The partially-sighted category, however, are able to use sighted methods that will be based on inkprint and type with the use of visual aids. Within either group there are also the other variations which one would expect to find in sighted children. There will be the clever and the dull, those whose handicap is part of a cerebral injury which affects them in other ways and children quite normal, except that they cannot see, or have severe visual defects. A child with little vision but good intelligence could appear to see much more than another who has better vision but less ability.

The blind

The widely held belief that other senses automatically become sharpened to compensate for the loss of sight, is just not true. Such ability for sensory substitution must nevertheless play a necessary part in the lives of those so afflicted and their education will be directed towards developing all the other senses to a higher degree. Opportunities are provided which can help not only to widen their sensory field but to assist them in the interpretation of experience. In addition, those who have little or no sight, unlike other handicapped pupils, must be able to recall the direction and extent of their movements. Basically this involves an education which will enable them to sift and classify incoming data efficiently from the four remaining senses. It is only when their movements become completely co-ordinated through constant exercise, that by feeling objects they may begin to build permanent mental pictures for themselves. However, among such a group are also some who have only an adequate motor system, coupled with an inability to conceive objects spatially, that will make learning extremely difficult.

In general, active and manipulative play using mobile toys, bead frames, pegs with peg-boards, wood blocks, salt and flour, can gradually be extended to creative activities which will involve many different materials, besides some use of simple tools. It is often useful to define clearly the space where the creative activity is carried out, as this will give some guidance to the hands and also help the child to keep track of the materials he is using; for when an article is out of reach, a blind child has no idea where to search. A large box-type tray may be used, that can contain both the work and materials needed. A work habit can then be developed in which both materials and activity are kept inside this boundary.

Materials which can be moulded or manipulated into relief and left to set hard have specific value for the blind, because this type of creation will enable pupils to retrace their hand and finger movements at a future time.

A blind pupil may learn the general outline and structure of a face by feeling his own features with the hands. When learning to model one, as in all situations, he must be encouraged to use any other helpful residual sense. In this instance, it could be an awareness of his own facial movements that will help him to model the features in their correct relationship.

The partially sighted

The visual handicaps of the partially sighted will include the following:

Defects in eye structure
Abnormal conditions
Defects in the visual fields
Defects in colour vision

Originally the setting up of separate schools for the partially sighted was to prevent an increase in myopia by preserving sight and also to meet the needs of those unable to cope within the ordinary educational system, yet who would not be classified as blind. Before the Second World War, pupils with high myopia were predominant and this determined the use of sight-saving methods throughout the whole curriculum in such schools, despite the fact that there were often other pupils who had some useful vision. These precautions were eventually proved to be of little purpose for myopia, since this is invariably an inherited optical defect in which the distance between lens and retina has increased because the eyeballs are longer than usual. This feature would therefore develop in the course of natural growth, despite external conditions.

Nowadays the myopes are less numerous in the schools for the partially sighted owing to the introduction of contact lenses. Instead, the greater proportion of these pupils will have congenital cataract, which may or may not be associated with myopia, and which is either hereditary or caused by the mother contracting German measles in early pregnancy. However, in both these groups will be found the cases with detached retina, and children with severe myopia are likely to develop this condition if care is not taken. The curriculum in the schools for the partially sighted thus avoids all activities which could cause violent jerks. This to some extent curtails the physical education programme, as there can be no high jump, leap-frogging or diving. In creative activity, too, hammering and the pounding method for preparing papier-mâché must be avoided.

There are conditions where vision is seriously impaired because a student is particularly sensitive to light. One of these is aniridia, in which absence of the iris means that the eye cannot adjust to light. Albinos also will be dazzled by ordinary light, for although the eyes are complete, they lack colour pigment. Contact lenses have proved useful for albinos, because not only do these reduce the light difficulty, but they are a cosmetic improvement. A student's sensitivity to light can be alleviated by providing tinted background papers for drawing and painting instead of white, which reflect the light more strongly.

Among the partially sighted are pupils who have congenital nystagmus, which causes the eyes to flutter; atrophy of the optic nerve; aphakia or absence of the lens; and micropthalmia, where the actual eye is small.

The visual field can be affected in several ways. In some cases, part of the visual field is missing and when this occurs on the same half with both eyes, a child will be blind on one side. The

'Figures'. Age 9 years. Retrolental fibroplasia. School for partially-sighted girls

macula is the sensitive centre of the retina. Any defect there can blur sight, although the periphery of the field may be normal. Those with macular degeneration therefore, are severely handicapped, for this is the most critical part of the visual field where all central vision can be lost.

There is one hereditary disease, retinitis pigmentosa, in which the area of blindness may circle the centre vision separating it from the peripheral field. This progressive condition can usually lead to blindness. Then there are defects of peripheral vision, such as the coloboma or fissure in the lens, iris, or retina, shaped like a keyhole, that has not closed over before birth and usually accounts for faults in the upper part of the visual field. There may be some cases also where the hyaloid artery that is present before birth does not become detached and remains in the path of vision.

A high proportion of blindness in children was due to a disturbance of the retina, called retrolental fibroplasia, which is now known to have been caused by the administration of too much oxygen to premature babies. Since oxygen concentrations have been restricted to below forty-five per cent, there is now a sharp decrease in the incidence of this condition.

Some partially-sighted pupils have visual disorders that may be progressive and eventually lead to blindness, but with most

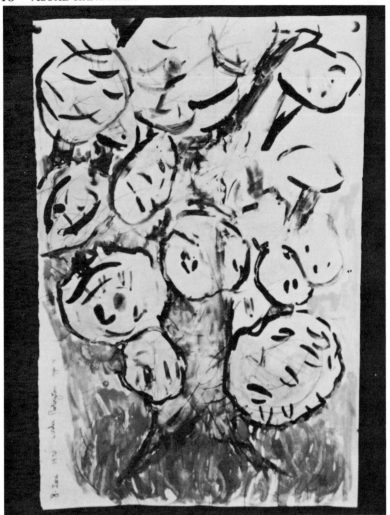

'Tree'. Age 9 years. Macular degeneration. School for partially-sighted girls

cases sight will remain limited. Although vision at long or middle distance is poor and performance that makes any of the finer demands on sight is difficult, they are able to find their way around and to cope with personal daily routines.

In their general training, emphasis is placed on teaching them to use whatever sight they have in all situations. The habit of using even limited vision will often help those who otherwise tend to grope their way about as if they were blind and where others, after mislaying objects close at hand, invariably conclude that these are either irretrievable or stolen.

The partially sighted are also encouraged to visualize things which are even beyond their field of vision. A group of partially-sighted girls were thus able to make paintings of the trees which grew around their boarding school, although their various visual defects prevented them from actually seeing these in their entirety. A mental picture had first to be built, so a start was made through bark rubbing and printing with leaves. The general structure and growth of a tree could then be conveyed by encouraging them to extend their arms and fingers, that they might realize all this through such movements.

The partially sighted are prisoners within a limited visual field. Creative activities must help them develop maximum sensitivity in the hands and fingers, besides a better co-ordination of body movement, that they may derive the fullest experience from the immediate environment and, by so doing, extend their knowledge of the world beyond the visual barriers.

Colour blindness

Colour blindness is probably due to a deficiency in the cells of the retina, making it unresponsive to the stimulation of primary colours. It is much more common than has generally been realized, occurring to an appreciable extent in one person out of fifty and more frequently among boys than girls. One boy in twelve will be colour blind to some degree.

The most common form is red–green blindness which will range from those who have only some minor degree of colour loss, such as when viewing objects at a distance or in poor light, to others for whom bright green and red are quite indistinguishable. In some cases the red, orange, yellow and green of the spectrum are seen as one colour, green, with the blue and violet both blue, while the bluish-green section will appear only a gap.

It will not always be easy for the adult to discover whether a child is colour blind merely by looking at the work produced, for the more intelligent become adept at covering up such defects. One girl with macular degeneration was colour blind but able to paint her tree in the conventional colours because she had asked her neighbour to show her the green and the brown in the palette beforehand. I have, however, seen a startling portrait produced by a colour blind fourteen-year-old boy in the life class. He had unwittingly painted the flesh violet and the eyes green, to the utter amazement of all. This was, of course, an extreme case, though even so the defect had passed unnoticed for years – as, no doubt, with others who were only mildly affected by colour blindness. In extreme cases creating with colour can bring little pleasure and I can recall one such student who always preferred to work in black and white.

Auditory handicaps

The majority of children within this category will usually have had substantial defects of hearing from birth or will have acquired them very early in life. Although it is not always possible to determine the cause of their deafness, it can be due to hereditary and congenital factors. Certain conditions can give rise to congenital malformations in the developing embryo and cause damage to the auditory system.

Permanent damage can be caused during the pre-natal period by virus infections such as influenza, rubella (German measles) and congenital syphilis. Profound deafness in a child can be due to German measles caught by the mother during early pregnancy. Nerve deafness may also be the result of toxicity caused by her intake of alcohol or certain drugs, while progressive nerve deafness is sometimes associated with retinitis pigmentosa.

Brain damage around birth and jaundice that is the result of the rhesus factor probably accounts for about one third who will have a serious partial hearing loss. Auditory handicaps acquired later are generally the result of meningitis, encephalitis, complications after measles or neglected middle-ear infections. Any of these factors may cause children to be handicapped in other ways.

The deaf child is unable to link his experiences with either language or sounds, unless this handicap was developed at a later stage when some concepts might already have been acquired. Those who are deaf do not necessarily have a total auditory loss and in fact this is rarely the case. In theory, therefore, as most deaf children possess a degree of residual hearing, it should be possible to help them receive some sound by means of electronic aids, excepting when there is damage within the perceptive mechanism of the brain which prevents the interpretation of any sounds, even though they may be transmitted normally.

Deafness can result when there are areas within the normal frequency range of sound that cannot be heard. Since only the lower frequencies register vowel sounds and consonants will be much higher, the learning difficulties concerned with the understanding and acquirement of speech must be commensurate to the distribution and variation in hearing loss throughout the entire range. Only when loss is slight and evenly distributed can words be understood that are spoken loudly, while even so, progress will be slow.

It will be realized that when children are handicapped in the basic means of communication, there is a real need for self-expression, particularly through art and craft activities in which they can perform on equal terms with others. Deaf children

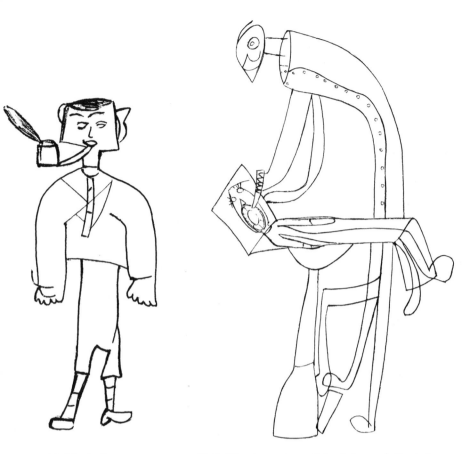

'A Man'. Boy, age 12 years. Retinitis pigmentosa. School for maladjusted deaf children. This deaf and partially-sighted pupil has also had the left eye removed. His drawing would suggest that he is perceptually specially sensitive to differences in the eyes and ears, because of his own handicaps

Age 11 years. School for maladjusted deaf children. Drawing by a girl following a visit to the dentist. She has brain damage, is deaf and cannot talk, but uses specific noises to express her pleasure or disapproval

however, will generally have a less developed sense of rhythm because their sensory experience lacks the recurring cadence of sounds, and since they do not hear the sound of their own foot-steps, even the movements in walking may be ungainly. They will seldom acquire a sense of rhythm to the same degree as ordinary children unless given remedial training. It may be that some will acquire a certain rhythm sense by observing the diversity of movements in their environment, providing that they have a well-developed visual orientation, while most of the profoundly deaf can at least feel vibrations and are taught to sense rhythms through developing their tactile perception. Printing and other creative activities which can help to develop a feeling for rhythm will therefore be particularly valuable.

The emphasis on rhythm experience in the education of the deaf not only increases their sensory awareness in this direction, but will also help them to develop better co-ordination of body movement generally. Since they may then more readily associate rhythm with the speech that is acquired, this too may be improved.

The fact that many deaf children are only able to hear sound in mutilated form, while others do not receive or cannot interpret it, will cause varying degrees of mental retardation. This makes any educational progress difficult, besides creating emotional problems that could result in some pupils developing grossly disturbed behaviour or even becoming completely withdrawn. Therefore, when teaching a group of maladjusted deaf pupils, it may often become necessary to achieve creativity while maintaining a damped-down atmosphere.

Art education for any maladjusted pupils, either with or without physical handicap, can provide a vital outlet for their emotional tensions, in which even unhealthy feelings can eventually be eradicated through this opportunity to express them through some creative means. Among the maladjusted are those who will frequently display a vindictive attitude towards other people. One maladjusted deaf boy, for instance, modelled quite realistic heads of two members of staff, so that these could be used to swear at whenever he felt inclined. Drawing was used by another to depict the crucifixion of all those with authority over him, and also a girl pupil whom he disliked.

It is because they have a feeling of insecurity and an inability to make satisfactory relationships with others, that many of the maladjusted deaf pupils are able to draw freely only when they can use the blackboard. Some of these children are more inclined to express themselves then, in the knowledge that they have the power to remove at will all traces of such effort. An outlet is thus provided for those who cannot commit themselves to any form of expression which can be shared by others.

Creative activity can give pupils a means to express mood or areas of anxiety and help them come to terms with life situations, something which is particularly important for those who lack speech.

Autism

Little is known about the medical and psychological aspects of the psychotic child or of the educational methods best suited to him, yet the incidence of psychosis in childhood is more prevalent than blindness and nearly as common as deafness. Although in the past psychotic children were diagnosed as severely subnormal or defective, it had also been recognized for a long time that there were differences which were sometimes indicated by their self-isolation and withdrawal, or severe learning difficulties, not infrequently accompanied by abilities that would be relatively normal or even above average.

It is now realized that these children might benefit from an educational environment which could offer them some suitable stimulation. This might be achieved by providing them with the means for self-expression through which they may realize some relationship with materials to help break down their isolation. It might involve them in the mastery of a simple tool, such as a hammer used for tapping down shapes to impress the surface of a thin metal sheet, or making models of animals to project their interests beyond themselves. One psychotic girl at a subnormality hospital also showed the typical features of perseverance in her rather stereotyped models of dogs which she always made with her lumps of clay. The chain in this activity was eventually broken of her own accord, when she attempted to model the speech therapist taking her dog for a walk. This creation differed from any normal interpretation of the subject, in that the therapist was modelled with a back view only.

In the present state of knowledge, it is not really certain whether in fact the term 'childhood psychosis', used when referring to all kinds of psychotic disorders, can be defined as a single condition, or if these children belong to as heterogeneous a group as those in any other handicap category. Some authorities on the subject have nevertheless attempted to isolate a classic form of the condition which is called 'autism'.

There is much literature available relative to all the research that has been done in the field of autism during recent years and inevitably many different and often conflicting views have been expounded. Despite the accumulation of a great deal of interesting and useful material, the amount of evidence available can but offer tentative conclusions on the subject. As yet, even the causes of autism remain a matter for conjecture and divergent theories have been put forward on each aspect of behaviour in autistic children while trying to discover whether it constitutes the basic defect or is a secondary factor.

These different opinions concerning aetiology can be hardly surprising when one realizes that autism is a state in which many if not all means for arousal and response can be impaired. Since the autistic child has multiple handicaps in which functions are not only underdeveloped but also distorted, this makes it both difficult for him to organize the incoming sensory material meaningfully, so that he may interpret the environment, or to communicate in any way. It is a condition more prevalent in boys than girls, usually beginning in early infancy or occasionally during the second year, and such a child will fail to develop normal use and understanding of language.

Before mentioning some forms of behaviour that can be observed in autistic children, it should be pointed out that no child will show all of these at any stage and many of them could be more accurately described as having features of autism in varying degree. Each of these is fairly common at some stage of their development and although they occur briefly in normal and much younger children, patterns of such behaviour can remain with the autistic for years.

Many autistic children are physically attractive and move gracefully, while they seem also to possess plenty of small finger movement. One nine-year-old boy at a junior training centre, for instance, would spend considerable time each day plucking at the curtains in the class-room, and on one occasion had stayed in the nearby patio until he had removed each petal from every flower on a bush. Like many autistic children he would frequently stand twisting his fingers to one side of the face or periphery of vision.

In their activities such children often show a preference for material in motion rather than that which is stationary, because they are able to recognize moving objects more readily. There are some who display a particular interest in sand or water, when the activity invariably consists of watching it trickle through their fingers, while they particularly like to see it drop from a height. Others will spin disks and watch them in motion. It is noticeable throughout most of these activities that they will often tilt the head in order to obtain various angle views, using peripheral vision instead of direct observation that might enable them to notice finer details.

It is probably their difficulty in making sense out of visual stimuli which accounts for the way these children seem to avoid looking one in the eye. The presence of visual dysfunctions may often cause them to seek additional stimuli for identifying objects, by smelling or even licking them or by tapping surfaces as though they were blind.

Autistic children can become obsessed by certain stimuli, which they will often seek voraciously. One boy, for instance, would never walk down the stairs without first stopping to see the light shining on the highly-polished handrail or pass the sink that was situated beneath a window without turning on the tap to look through the running stream of water. Even in the dining-hall he never failed to hold the red or blue plastic drinking glasses up to the light. Some, on the other hand, may collect certain things, seeking a particular shape or colour. One sixteen-year-old girl had developed an obsession for pink objects and would usually be seen clutching some of these, which included a collection of small cushions and dolls without clothes. On one occasion she tried to snatch for her collection a pink jumper that was being worn by another pupil. A further example of this obsessive behaviour was shown through her insistence upon arranging the family toothbrushes, not only to place them in a particular order, but so that they were all facing one way.

The fanatical adherence to certain routines is typical of many autistic pupils and probably stems from their attempts to use continually only those codes which they have already understood from an environment that to them is still overwhelming with its complex patterns. It is noticeable that when some simple skill has been acquired, they tend to repeat this rather than develop it further and will resist any attempts made to teach them anything new.

'Sad and happy painting'. Girl, age 7 years. School for the autistic

'Elongated painting'. Girl, age 9 years. School for the autistic

Autistic children might seem to be deaf because they do not respond to speech or noise, particularly if it is of a loud and sudden kind, yet some will become absorbed in small sounds, while others even enjoy music. Such contradictory evidence would support the theory that response is dependent upon cognition, and the auditory defects of autistic children might be accounted for by their inability to comprehend sounds. There will be no reaction, therefore, to noises that they do not understand.

If these children are not helped, many will remain withdrawn or become more disturbed and difficult to manage. Days could be spent rocking back and forth, biting their wrists or banging their heads, for self-inflicted injuries are a feature which distinguishes the autistic condition from other psychiatric disorders.

The severity of their defects which can prevent them from organizing incoming stimuli of all kinds, presents a tremendous challenge to a teacher's ingenuity. Since most children, however, show some kind of sensory exploration, this might provide a clue as to how individual teaching may be introduced. The child's obsessions could also become the basis of occupation which will eventually lead him to more purposeful activity. This is demonstrated by the case of a nine-year-old girl who seemed absorbed only in her own fingers. Blobs of water colour and nail varnish were painted on her nails in the hope that she would come to match these with similarly coloured beads also provided. Within six months she was contentedly pressing down beads in areas of each colour on to a Plasticine surface.

One very intelligent seven-year-old autistic girl who at five years of age had been the eldest of four children, could eventually express her depressed moods through painting. She invariably used certain symbols to express them, such as faces with drooping mouths and little figures always pushing against big brown mountains. Gradually she began to paint both happy and sad facial expressions side by side.

Another girl, aged nine and a half years, had learned to read although she showed difficulties in comprehension, while her paintings indicated some perceptual disorder. One could always pick out her work from the rest, since it was distinguishable by the elongation of all form. Even human hair would be shown growing upwards and everything leaned away from the horizontal.

Brain damage

Anything which will impede the natural pattern of growth for any organ in a developing embryo can cause serious defects, while damage could otherwise occur during birth, immediately afterwards, or as the result of an illness later. Since there are certain common factors which will cause interference with normal development of the heart, eyes, ears, limbs or brain, more than one handicap might result. A brain-damaged child can therefore be multiply handicapped, although this is not inevitable.

Cerebral palsy

Cerebral palsy is essentially damage to those parts of the brain which control co-ordination of muscular activity. Brain damage produces motor handicaps, causing these children to move abnormally, while other less obvious handicaps may exist besides, which will create certain learning difficulties that are found also in other brain-damaged children.

Children who have cerebral palsy may be classified according to the type of movement which they show and by the distribution of motor disorders in the body, although experience will prove that these are not always so clearly defined. It will be helpful, however, if one can identify classic examples of these, such as the muscular incoordination of ataxia that is due to damage of the cerebellum and recognizable by the staccato drunken gait, or the involuntary writhing muscle activity associated with athetosis. In both of these conditions, the whole body tends to be affected.

It has become quite common practice to call those who have cerebral palsy 'spastics', although strictly this is a term only applicable to one group. Spasticity is a form of paralysis where the affected muscles are permanently tightened up in contraction, a condition which affects the largest group within the cerebral palsy category. Here one may recognize the lop-sided posture of hemiplegics, when left or right side is affected and others whose hands appear more useful than their legs, besides the quadriplegics in which spasticity affects all four limbs.

It becomes apparent from these observations alone that the needs of all these children could vary according to the type of movement they possess. In general terms this would seem to range from an abnormal excess of movement, down to small weak action in one or two fingers only. But this does not take into account the possibility of any other disabilities that, together, can severely handicap those who may otherwise appear to be only mildly disabled.

It may not be the obvious physical handicap, therefore, that

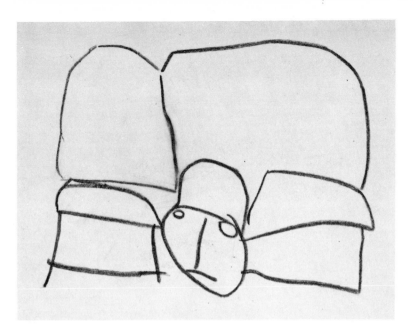

'Policeman'. Age 7 years. School for partially-sighted girls. Toxoplasmosis infection during pregnancy can cause brain damage in the newborn, or abortion. There was no register of I.Q. for this girl due to her lack of verbal ability

'Policeman'. Age 10 years. School for partially-sighted girls. This girl suffered a lack of oxygen at birth and has brain damage and cataracts, although her twin is quite normal. During birth there is a greater risk that the second twin may be deprived of oxygen

could provide the biggest obstacle to learning, but rather the mixture of disabilities, which creates a formidable barrier to the acquirement of knowledge. Brain damage leaves these children with uncoordinated movement, where in some cases even the act of swallowing may have to be consciously controlled, and

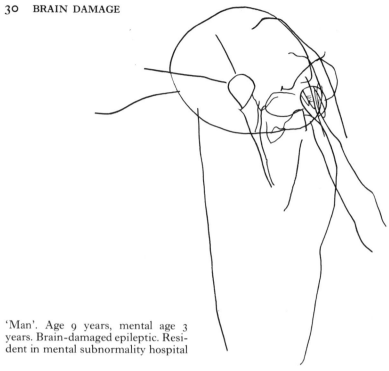

'Man'. Age 9 years, mental age 3 years. Brain-damaged epileptic. Resident in mental subnormality hospital

'Policeman'. Age 8 years. School for partially-sighted girls. This girl has congenital cataracts which leave her with practically tunnel vision. This is an example of the damage that can be caused by the administration of too much oxygen to a premature baby

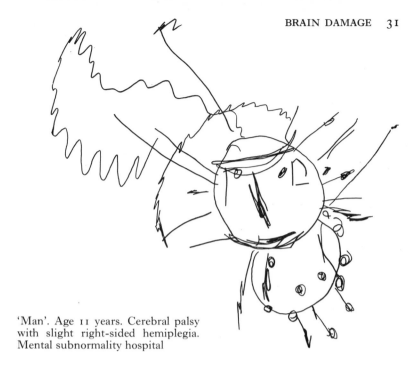

'Man'. Age 11 years. Cerebral palsy
with slight right-sided hemiplegia.
Mental subnormality hospital

because they suffer a disorganized body mechanism, their
sensory powers may be impaired. They could also lack any
natural feeling for rhythm. There might be deafness, as is
particularly the case with athetoids, while a defective sense of
touch, or sight and speech difficulties are prevalent. It is hardly
surprising that some will have an incomplete knowledge of body
image or lack all sense of distance and direction.

Although the athetoids could have some perceptual difficulties,
there is undoubtedly less visuo-motor disorder among them than
with spastics. It would appear that the spastics are more prone to
spatial disorders than the other two groups and have these in
varying degree, when some may not even know their own
relative position to the space around them. The kinaesthetic
sensation by which we are able to realize the position of trunk,
head or limbs, has various receptors within the inner ear, joints,
muscles and tendons, that in conjunction with the senses of
sight, hearing, touch and movement, help to provide us with the
necessary information about spatial relationships. In spastics,
this system has often been rendered ineffective through their
uncoordinated body mechanism.

Many of these children can develop the maximum use of any
hand and finger movements that they have, through activities
which involve learning to feel materials, shapes and rhythms. In
this way, not only are they helped to overcome specific physical
handicaps, but to derive some mental stimulus from their
movements and so improve muscular co-ordination. The
development of purposeful movement through repetitive performance is an essential factor in improving this relationship

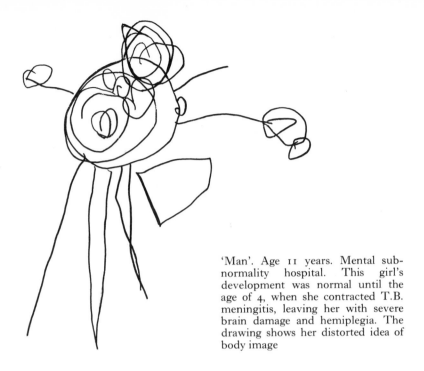

'Man'. Age 11 years. Mental sub-normality hospital. This girl's development was normal until the age of 4, when she contracted T.B. meningitis, leaving her with severe brain damage and hemiplegia. The drawing shows her distorted idea of body image

and it will be noticeable that as soon as some useful patterns of movement have been established, spastics can become quite enthusiastic in using them. It is by helping many of those who have cerebral palsy to build up their own personal movement patterns that they may gradually be taught to know themselves more fully and be able to start taking a lively interest in the environment. One thirteen-year-old spastic girl, severely handicapped and in a wheel-chair, had the use of only two fingers on one hand. Nevertheless she acquired the light rhythmic knack of working an embroidery and rug needle, which enabled her to create simple linear embroideries.

All activities will be based on simple sensory experience and are readily repeated by these children, primarily for the purely physical pleasure which this brings and then because it is possible for them to obtain tangible results. This is particularly noticeable in the case of hemiplegic boys who can be induced to make salt or balsa wood carvings with a file and to bring the affected hand into action through the sheer appeal which this activity has. A hand which has become useful to such a child is more readily employed, becoming more relaxed and normal in movement. In time, the movement which has been achieved by voluntary action and constant effort may become a reflex function, releasing mental energies for achieving real creativity.

It is by using the existing movement to the full that some stronger and more definite function is first established. Athetoids are therefore encouraged to create by practising their sweeping movements, or ataxics to stab down patterns.

Eventually they will be able to modify these movements and athetoids are then capable of working on a modified scale, while even ataxics have been known to become proficient in using the electric sewing-machine.

Many pupils can be helped towards making finer and more complex movements only if creative activities are selected specifically for bringing into use other parts of the hand or even an idle limb where this is at all possible. Hemiplegics, for instance, are encouraged to bring the affected side into action, which they would otherwise ignore. Often some normal function can be established in a handicapped limb by using it at every opportunity. Its use will help to improve posture and at the same time bring other creative experiences within the child's scope. Use of a handicapped limb can be achieved by providing activity which it is impossible to complete single-handed. One hemiplegic boy, aged thirteen years, was engaged in creating a large wall panel by pressing various bowls and lids on to a surface of papier-mâché and Polyfilla (Spackle) mixture. The suction created by this process made it necessary for him to use both hands in order to remove the objects from the surface so as to rearrange them, something he was only too eager to do because of his interest in the project.

In others, the type of motor handicap may not be so clearly defined and sometimes the lifting of an unused hand will cause a spasm which upsets all control of the other side. These are

Age 9 years. Cerebral palsy, quadriplegic. Special school. First drawings with a slip tracer by a boy without speech

obviously the cases where pupils should be helped in developing maximum movement of one hand only. Some, as they progress, become quite adept at devising ways of by-passing their disabilities in order to carry out an idea, which shows the great incentive and satisfaction that they derive from their own achievement.

Epilepsy

Epilepsy can be displayed either as *grand mal* fits, in which the child falls unconscious to the ground, or as *petit mal*, where consciousness may only lapse for a matter of seconds and could even pass unnoticed. An epileptic condition frequently occurs in combination with other handicaps and is due to a dysrhythmic function of the brain. It has been discovered that nerve energy of the normal brain can be expended suddenly and in an explosive but regulated manner under the control of will. The epileptic, however, has a disposition to excessive excitability of the brain, which causes an uncontrolled and abnormal discharge of energy to occur at intervals. There are inherited factors that could give a predisposition to this excitability, while it may be caused by injury at birth, or as the result of an accident.

Drugs are used for the control of fits, but since the type and dosage for an epileptic attending special school will be varied from time to time, this can cause the behaviour or educational achievement to fluctuate accordingly. Although this treatment may actually prevent a fit from occurring, some epileptic pupils are liable to outbursts of destructive behaviour or will make sudden and unprovoked attacks on others.

It is believed that when epileptics become absorbed in an activity they may be less likely to have a fit, and so art education should provide them with a variety of interests. Violent outbursts may often be averted in others if at the first sign of restless behaviour they are given those creative processes which involve plenty of physical activity.

Spina bifida and hydrocephalus

The protrusion of spinal membranes through a fissure, due to developmental defect in the lower part of the spine, is known as spina bifida. Those children so affected may have complete paralysis of the legs and are often incontinent. Quite frequently there might also be a blockage in the circulation of cerebrospinal fluid, so that this accumulates within the brain. Hydrocephalus is the condition where an abnormal accumulation of fluid in the cerebral ventricles or subarachnoid space of the brain can cause enlargement of the skull, severe brain damage and convulsions.

Although it has been suggested that one may expect an increase in the number of pupils with spina bifida, there is a chance now that, for many, early surgery can do much to preserve normal function in the legs or make some mobility possible. The insertion of a Spitz-Holter valve at the base of the skull to syphon off the excess cerebro-spinal fluid has also helped to arrest or reduce dramatically the development of gross hydrocephalus as seen in the past.

A small number of these children will have brain damage of a general or specific kind, which is either due to developmental injury or pressure from hydrocephalus and although there will be others whose paralysis still exists, many within this category can be regarded as physically handicapped pupils of normal intelligence.

Like all handicapped children, they have a need for personal achievement which will help to build their self-confidence. It is noticeable that while they may develop some strong hand movements, the moving of separate fingers can often prove difficult. Modelling activities in clay, plasticine and papier-mâché mixtures provide a wide variety of hand and finger movements which would be suitable. Processes involving paper tearing, arrangements of small units such as in mosaic, or the use of the rug and embroidery needle will provide the exercise of smaller finger movements and the need for varied pressure.

Minimal brain damage

Sometimes a child's brain damage may be very slight or he may suffer some cerebral dysfunction for which no direct evidence can be found. Medical histories of those in this category will often reveal a high incidence of complications happening before, during or after birth. Many of these children are of average intelligence and will therefore be found in our ordinary schools, yet while they may appear at first to be quite normal, learning and behavioural difficulties become more obvious when they grow older.

Superficial evidence may assess these pupils as being clumsy, untidy, lazy, difficult, excitable and constantly overactive, or even mentally retarded. There is often evidence of limitations or delays in normal functions when, for example, they fail to execute the simple skills involved in dressing themselves at an appropriate age. Although there are a proportion below average intelligence, all may be suffering basically from lack of co-

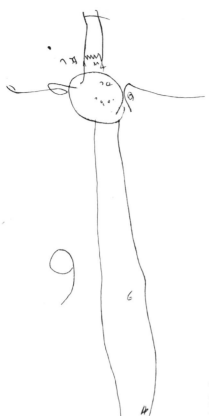

'Man'. Age 11 years, mental age $2-2\frac{1}{2}$ years. Minimal brain damage. Resident in mental deficiency hospital

ordination that is the result of a sensory or visuo-motor disability. This creates both educational and social problems for them that are far from minimal. Failure to recognize these problems could deprive them of the extra help which they may need and cause many to become emotionally disturbed.

Any skill which presents particular difficulty to an individual pupil should be noted, as it is often possible to analyse the movement patterns that are involved and to use these as the bases for a series of therapeutic activities. It is sometimes necessary to break down a skill into simpler parts so that each may be learned separately. One eleven-year-old boy seemed to lack the normal mobility in his fingers needed to tie his own shoelaces and tie. Exercises for inducing greater flexibility of the fingers were given as he wound strings in all directions to make structures on a picture frame which had nails round all four sides. Winding and twisting medium-gauge iron wire into abstract constructions also helped him to feel the direction of his finger movements.

Repetition is an essential part of the therapy and not only does art activity provide an interesting way of using this, but it also makes it possible for children to build up the patterns and memories of movements which are essential to the performance of any motor function. When this can be linked with some creative achievement, it will also help to eradicate the child's feeling of inadequacy and restore morale.

Brain dysfunctions

There are complex learning disabilities associated with brain dysfunctions. One type has been defined as agnosia, where the information received by the auditory, visual or tactual senses cannot be interpreted. This is often confined to one sensory pathway so that the pupil is unable to comprehend through the defective channel. A child with visual agnosia, for instance, will not recognize objects by sight but may be taught initially through another sense and perhaps learn instead to identify these by touch.

Sometimes a pupil finds it extremely difficult and even impossible to manipulate objects or carry out an intended movement although he has no motor disability. This learning disability is known as apraxia.

It is the disorders of perception, however, that are more comprehensive in effect, since they are responsible for a fundamental distortion of total experience.

The term 'brain damage', which at first might seem to suggest the identification of some well-defined syndrome will, in fact, cover a wide variety of conditions, depending upon which part of the brain has been affected. It can handicap movement, impair the kinaesthetic sense and cause failure in those parts which interpret the messages obtained by sight, hearing or sensation, besides affecting the areas that are associated with intelligence. Even an eye defect such as a squint could be relative to brain dysfunction and it has also been suggested that in mentally retarded children this may be partly the reason why some fail to make skilled movements.

Failure in adjustment to life situations and the attendant behavioural problems that may result, could be due to the adaptive difficulties arising from such disabilities, particularly if there is no specific training directed towards improving the situation. Here creative activity can be used to exploit any movements through which these children are most able to comprehend their experience and may even help in stimulating a weaker sense. A ten-year-old girl who was partially sighted and deaf was introduced to rhythmic painting and printing activities in order primarily to extend her scale of work beyond a limited field of vision. A marked improvement in her deportment showed that this had also aroused a critical awareness of rhythm in body movement.

Mental retardation

The assessment of I.Q. in a multiply handicapped child can prove difficult during the early years since the various aspects of this condition can often prevent or restrict any application of intelligence in direct form. The task of differentiating between primary and secondary features that can help one to discover whether impairment is basically due to a physical or mental cause, will also be by no means easy. Whatever the final result eventually proves, the multiply handicapped child cannot reveal his full potential and functions initially at a mentally retarded level. It therefore becomes necessary for the teacher to work from a profile of each child that is based upon observation of both negative and positive functioning over the field of visuo-motor control, perceptual and manipulative ability and powers of communication, besides such expressions of behaviour as concentration or self-control.

The basic means for establishing contact with these children can often be found by introducing carefully selected creative activities where the exercise of one particular sense may help in stimulating others. Not only can they provide essential movement therapy, but also opportunity for pupils to admire their own creative efforts, thus giving them the necessary incentive to repeat these. At the same time, any progress or setback which occurs will add valuable data that may help to clarify the real difficulties in learning which they might have. A quadriplegic ten-year-old boy, for example, encountered difficulty in focusing his eyes at crucial moments. He was helped considerably to overcome this by learning to feel the rhythmic printing of patterns, since during such periods he had learned to synchronize both his body movements and focus in order to be able to place each print accurately.

Apart from those pupils where underfunctioning is primarily due to physical handicaps, there are many children who are mentally subnormal besides being physically handicapped or autistic and the mental subnormality can be qualitatively the same as in any other child. Many types of mental retardation, however, can occur without any physical disability and it is understandable that human nature has been slower in showing the same sympathy towards this category as it extends to those who are physically handicapped. This is probably because the effects cannot easily be assessed in obvious terms like a deformed arm or leg, and since the tragic implications of such a handicap are not easily understood, a physically able-bodied human being who can make but inadequate or abnormal response to ordinary situations does not necessarily evoke the same sentiment.

The differences between a normal and subnormal child are basically those which concern level of intelligence and development. It may also be necessary to differentiate between those whose mental retardation is due to low intelligence and others who only function at mental subnormality level through some emotional disturbance. Mental subnormality may not be entirely due to an innate intelligence factor, for a closer link between emotion and learning exists than is generally appreciated.

Emotional factors
One theory would suggest that there are optimal learning periods in early childhood for acquiring certain functions, such as the comprehension of sounds, learning to talk and acquirement of basic habits. Some of the vital groundwork for all future learning is irretrievably lost if this natural course of progress is disrupted by psychological stress. Any unfavourable conditions could cause this to happen, such as a spell in hospital or an addition to the family. If it occurs at a critical point the learning process may not be resumed when once the optimal period is passed.

Personality development is based upon the security of family relationships which are established during this early period. Where physically handicapped children have been subject to frequent spells in hospital for treatment or surgery during the pre-school years, their personal drive and motive might then prove difficult to activate, with the result that progress in learning could be retarded.

Lack of parental love and understanding too may have the effect of handicapping a child not only emotionally but intellectually so that he is unable to attain his full potential, as this deprivation in his existence may destroy all purpose for personal achievement. A child thus rejected can become so maladjusted that he is even unable to form any satisfactory relationships with others. Since emotional factors can result in both passive and aggressive maladaptive attitudes to life situations, emotionally disturbed children may either become apathetic pupils or difficult to manage with their unpredictable moods and behaviour. It is only by helping to strengthen their ego that one may gradually lead them towards a greater acceptance of reality. Education must provide conditions in which their interest can be stimulated and creative activities will be required that could develop a greater self-awareness in many ways.

The normal child may obtain inspiration for his creativity

even from vicarious experiences, but art methods with those who are mentally retarded are generally most successful when they are focused on the pupil's own personal experiences. An initial approach is therefore based upon creative activities which are physically stimulating and introduce a wide variety of sensory experiences and repetitive movement through which the children will gain a fuller physical awareness of themselves. Furthermore, ideas that are presented for creativity of a representational kind may be such that a child can identify himself with the subject, since some appeal to his egoism will usually arouse most enthusiasm.

An awareness of self is perhaps best demonstrated when children who are past the symbolic stage of drawing and painting will invariably depict people with a definite resemblance to their own physical features. For example, one fifteen-year-old E.S.N. boy had a noticeably small head and his pictures of both humans and animals were distinguishable by their having this particular feature. Some severely maladjusted deaf pupils, however, were creatively unresponsive to the colour and spectacle seen during their visit to the circus, because they were unable to regard this experience as anything more than a passing scene that was quite apart from themselves. This attitude will also be found among many who are mentally retarded.

'Daddy'. Age 10 years. Mongolism, S.S.N. Junior training centre

The subnormal child is particularly sensitive to anything which he considers might be lowering to his status. The moods which this causes will be frankly shown because he is less inhibited than the normal pupil. Therefore even small incidents in his daily life can cause both his behaviour and his achievement to be so variable that steady progress is sometimes impossible.

Many become only too aware of their past failures and it often becomes necessary, if any educational progress is to be made, to take steps in order to desensitize those areas of experience which could evoke any such emotional threat. Quite often this failure will be due to continual presentation of a medium which gives no satisfaction to the child. A pupil knows, for instance, that his paintings are a mess because he always fails to control the paint on his brush. Instead of being content to repeat past failures, he may eventually react to this particular activity with a display of anti-social behaviour. This is a situation which will frequently be recognized in the lower first year streams of the secondary modern school. The introduction of some new approach to the subject in which paint could be applied in other ways might resolve the situation and enable a child who is so disturbed to experience instead a feeling of quiet achievement.

Art can be used to help treat personality disturbances by providing activities in which a child can succeed at his own speed and with materials often chosen by himself. Sometimes the fear that unfavourable comparisons can be made with reality will deter a pupil from attempting any representational creation. He may then find self-expression in producing work of a purely abstract kind through learning to exploit the varied nature of different media. One rather timid E.S.N. girl, at thirteen years old, suddenly displayed considerable creative ability when she became absorbed in colour and texture for creating her fabric collages. There should be, therefore, a range of activities to choose from, so that different forms of creativity will be going on within the one room. In this way a freer and more stimulating atmosphere is at once established, where each pupil can experiment with different tools and materials.

It is the opportunity for personal achievement that comes from learning to manipulate simple tools or control materials which helps to boost the ego and compensate for failures in other channels. Creative activities are valuable as they not only have the power to calm but also provide for the emotions positive outlets that will help a child to build up confidence and self-respect. One thirteen-year-old boy from the lowest stream of a secondary school, already beyond parental control and in the care of a children's home, could find all this through carving in chalk. Although much of this success will be based upon individual achievement, art education for the mentally retarded should also provide opportunities where pupils can participate in projects involving teamwork as part of the therapy, because it is this particular aspect which can do much to bring about their personal and social adjustment.

Environmental deprivation

The development of intelligence in any child may depend considerably upon the stimulation which he receives from his environment during the pre-school years. A child may be deprived of valuable sensory experiences through his surroundings alone, which can cause him to become educationally subnormal. This will often occur where the pupil comes from a large family which has low cultural standards. Such a situation is not necessarily due to any accepted forms of material deprivation, for it frequently occurs in our modern affluent society where young children are often cooped up in tall blocks of modern flats in our towns and cities to gaze down upon the surrounding desert of concrete blocks and tarmac. Sensory deprivation can also result where home ceases to be the hub of stimulating activities, because life is centred on continuous and indiscriminate television viewing. These factors can deprive a child at a time when he should be gaining important first-hand experiences and the deprivation could affect his educational progress as seriously as a mental or physical handicap which prevents others obtaining stimulation from the environment. It is vital, therefore, that art education for all these children should be based upon simple creative activities that will increase their physical and mental awareness of the world around them.

Theories now indicate that an inability to understand spatial relationships plays a significant part in creating learning difficulties with the three R's, regardless of I.Q. Thus we may find many handicapped children of average or higher intelligence who find difficulty in acquiring these basic skills on which much of the ordinary education is developed, while some pupils with I.Qs in the sixties are well-endowed in these particular requirements for learning to read and write to a standard that could be acceptable in ordinary schools. Some research also suggests that the structure of logical thinking probably does not evolve through language, but might rather be the result of co-ordinated actions transformed into thought.

Mental retardation is not merely a matter of limited intelligence

'House'. Age 14 years. Mongolism,
S.S.N. Junior training centre

but could be determined by unfavourable physical, emotional
or environmental conditions. It would seem that an art
curriculum directed towards developing the responses to tactual
experiences, with a clearer definition of movement, direction,
rhythm and spatial relationships, could help to supplement
other areas of learning.

Educable subnormals have been regarded as those children
who fall below 75 I.Q. with the number of pupils above,
officially, very small. No hard and fast rule determining the
point for a special school education at either end can be fixed in
practice, since it will be realized that there are factors which
have to be taken into account in making any assessment of
mentally retarded children that do not rest on I.Q. alone.

It is usual to stimulate creativity in pupils at ordinary schools
by presenting them with suitable subjects which they can
express through the various media. While some of the
educationally subnormal may also respond to this method, the
art curriculum for the severely subnormal will be entirely
devoted to motivating their activity through the aspects of
concrete learning experience.

Down's syndrome (mongolism)

In this group will be pupils with Down's syndrome, named after
Dr John Langdon-Down, who defined the characteristics as far

back as 1866, although it is perhaps more generally known by the term 'mongolism', because these children have an inward slant of the eyes which tends to give them an oriental appearance. Other obvious features will include a flattened skull and short, small fingers.

It was not until the late 1950s that abnormalities in the chromosomal factor were identified in these children, for instead of possessing the usual forty-six chromosomes, they have an extra one, which is either quite distinct or sometimes attached to another. Since similar abnormal chromosome patterns have been found in only some of the parents, such evidence as to whether mongolism is hereditary still remains inconclusive. There is, however, a possibility that this particular abnormality may be a direct result of some infection before birth.

While children with Down's syndrome may be severely subnormal, others are less so. It has been suggested that the deficit which they have as a result of their small cerebellum might cause them to be poor in shape recognition by touch, or at copying shapes, but they possess a flexibility in the joints which gives them an abnormally wide range and elasticity of movement. Mongols are often notoriously good at imitation too, and this probably helps to give them a certain social maturity which might seem inconsistent with their actual mental level. It is not surprising that the mongol pupils could take the initiative in performing various simple routines during the dancing class at a junior training centre. Another ten-year-old pupil always made a point of adding his age and also six symbols for the letters of his name to all his drawings, although these would vary in shape each time.

Occasionally mongols learn to read and write a bit, while most of them usually have a happy disposition which enables them to adapt easily to the class-room situation. Reaction to new impressions may be slow, but many respond to training in the performance of simple repetitive skills. They do, however, have behavioural traits which are in some respects stereotyped. One mongol, for instance, was trained by his father to remove the ashtrays and empty glasses from the tables in a club, which he could do most efficiently, but when the drinking licence had been extended for a particular event, nothing would induce him to stop performing this accustomed routine at the usual time. Even at S.S.N. level, where I.Q. scores will range between 30 and 55, the constant effort required by repetition of movements in creative activity will help to increase maximum finger manipulation and manual dexterity that could be the basis for learning simple industrial skills later. Since so many factory occupations will demand such skills as matching and assembling objects, much valuable practice through creative activity can be given by encouraging the child to attempt to place a variety of materials in particular positions. They should have considerable practice in arranging these into some order and should be encouraged to enjoy the repetition of shape that can be linked with their own body movements. Often pupils may be further helped by being provided with tangible ways of working out visuo-spatial relationships.

More recent research on the subject would suggest that, given short periods of individual tuition with even complex material, it is possible for the mentally handicapped to do better than the levels of skill generally expected from them. Differences between the S.S.N. and those with normal intelligence was not so much a matter of what they could eventually learn, but of the time this took to achieve.

Some guiding principles

Since the handicapped have a diversity of intellectual, emotional or physical characteristics and because the complexities caused by an assortment of different disabilities may occur in any individual, therapy must cover many aspects. Basic learning experiences are non verbal, sensation experience being the most primitive form, and it is possible in many cases to start the therapy through activities which can make some appeal at this level.

Before the normal child goes to school, much learning has already taken place in an informal way through his own activities, learning which cannot be acquired by many who are handicapped. It is important therefore that much of the creative activity should fulfil the handicapped child's special need for direct contact with materials. Sensory deprivation can be reversed in some cases by the introduction of commonplace substances, including both natural and even discarded man-made material, through which one may induce some tactile stimulation. At the same time, emphasis should be laid upon providing activities which will bring pupils maximum opportunity for experiencing either direct sensations of movement or other sensations gained through the use of unorthodox tools.

There is the need to develop the residual senses of the blind and deaf along similar lines; that they may become the compensatory means to their learning and adjustment. In some conditions of severe physical or mental handicap, knowledge cannot be acquired through visual appeal and all educational progress may depend on whether a teacher can help children establish patterns of movement besides the finer finger movements that will also help to increase their mental awareness. It is therefore essential to ensure that each activity will be carried out on a scale which proves adequate for the type of movements required. In the case of certain physical handicaps, one may have to relate this to the posture or abnormal movements that the child already has.

It is becoming increasingly apparent that opportunities and incentives for creative pastimes in childhood are sadly neglected in a modern urban environment and that art education must provide all pupils with creative activities which can improve their tactual sensitivity, that they may learn to understand and enjoy artistic creation and awareness.

Many of the creative activities suggested for the handicapped will be applicable to normal children, but when introducing them to children with handicaps, there is often the greater problem of bridging the gap between teaching and spontaneous application. It is perhaps only when one is faced with both a practical subject and a handicapped child that the extent to which learning processes are dependent upon movement will be fully appreciated. Initially it is through establishing some purposeful movement that the handicapped can develop a means for spontaneous creativity. This makes it important that any movements acquired should be directed towards a worthwhile conclusion in order to maintain the child's interest for further effort. It is during these early stages that any success in this direction will also help to establish a happy relationship between pupil and teacher, upon which all future progress in learning might depend. The actual course which the creative activity will follow cannot be forecast as it is peculiar to each individual pupil. While one may anticipate further achievement through one particular channel, this will be by no means certain and makes it essential to have an alternative programme ready, should this fail. The procedure subscribes to a theory that where one channel is closed, an appeal made through another may enable the learning process to continue. This means that the creative activities must be closely linked with purposeful bodily movement in order to help them attain a greater sensitivity to the immediate environment.

Failure may in fact be due to dysfunction at a higher level of basic learning experience that involves perceptual ability. It is this which enables the pupil not only to discriminate among visual and auditory stimuli, but to organize every incoming sensation into a meaningful whole. Where there are pupils with visuo-perceptual disturbances, visual experiences are distorted and creative activities must be introduced which may be satisfactorily completed because they provide non-visual clues to guide the pupils in their spatial confusion. Suitable activities might well include arrangements of shapes within a well-defined area which enables the child to relate the units being placed with the outer edges he can feel. Those children who appear unable to distinguish form or shape visually may be helped if given textured units.

Failure to relate themselves to the surrounding space can also be due to some disturbance in pupils of their own body image. It may therefore prove necessary to help some pupils form a kinaesthetic image from the sequence of such movements as are required in performing any simple process. These pupils must learn to associate sensation with each movement that they make and during the initial stages, this might only be achieved by the teacher actually manipulating a child's hand and fingers in some positive direction or imposing manual pressure upon a tentative effort at closing the hands round solid shapes or modelling material.

Quite often many of those who are physically handicapped must learn all these experiences while confined to a wheel-chair, which means that considerable thought is necessary in the organization of materials. It is important that wherever possible these pupils should be able to experience periods of absolute independence and any extra effort which this might entail will be worthwhile, even though this can only result in a short period before things need to be rearranged. We may help many in this way to develop positive attitudes towards themselves that are important to mental health.

All materials should be prepared by the teacher beforehand. Meticulous organization is essential in preparing creative activities for all handicapped pupils, so that tools and materials will be at hand. This is because many have emotional or mental disabilities which make it necessary that negative feelings of frustration should be kept to a minimum in order that they might have a better chance of success. There is a particular need for self-achievement in children with learning difficulties, as through this they may experience the feeling that they have some control over their own environment. Sometimes art education will play an important part when the phobias or primitive anti-social drives of some pupils are directed through carefully selected activity so that they may be released in a harmless or more productive way.

When children have never known the challenging and rewarding adventures that are experienced in the course of natural development, creative activities which involve a variety of materials should help them acquire physical skills and realize their basic emotional need for new experiences. The frustration of those who already know failure can be eradicated even within the same creativity area, through emphasizing a physical approach to provide them with fresh incentives. There are many pupils in our ordinary schools who find creative expression difficult when this particular aspect is not encouraged.

Both physical or mental handicap and even insecure environmental conditions alone can cause children to become detached or alienated from the world around them. Creative education can be a means for helping many to organize their experience and develop a better self-concept, that they may gradually extend their interests beyond themselves and become more socially adjusted.

Drawing

The normal young child, like the primitive, has an urgent desire to express himself in picture language, but although handicap can make this difficult or almost impossible, such evidence of free expression as one is able to obtain will often reveal some particular aspect of handicapped children's learning disabilities.

Their attempts at drawing the human figure are of particular value in this respect, where results may be very primitive and, not infrequently, extremely bizarre. Some may fail to produce an organized drawing of the human figure because they are unable to make spatial judgements and therefore have extreme difficulty in obtaining the correct spatial relationship of the body parts. This distortion may be a direct result of their having a faulty body image, for some handicapped children are unaware of all the parts of even their own body. Those with cerebral palsy, for instance, will often ignore the affected limb, while some autistic children are unable to localize a sensation.

When pupils are unaware of their personal identity despite personal grace and agility, as can happen in autism, it is possible that they could have an incomplete body image. It took three years of constant effort to teach a girl, aged ten years, to draw a figure. The teacher helped her each day to build a body image by touching the child's head, eyes and other appropriate parts, or rubbing each limb, while verbalizing each relationship.

Another aspect of the possession of a complete body image and its connection with self-perception is illustrated through the teaching of blind children. Here it has been noticed that only when this is directed towards giving them a body awareness will pronouns and the third person be used correctly. There are several conditions which could affect the body image of handicapped children, such as emotional disturbance, mental retardation, their own poor co-ordination in body movements, besides dysfunctions which include visuo-perceptual deficits.

It is interesting that spatial abnormalities will sometimes be revealed in the drawings of normal pupils. One is not of course alluding to the phase when young children, in following the course of natural development, will draw an aerial view, perhaps of a duck pond in the middle of a park scene, surrounded by perpendicular trees, but to spatial deviation which may show at a later stage.

A thirteen-year-old Sikh boy, for instance, who had mastered our language and produced elaborate illustrations of his country, only showed spatial deviation whenever he made drawings of the cattle he had helped to tend, by placing both eyes on the same side of the head. This particular abnormality will occasionally be found in animal drawings by secondary school pupils.

Drawing on wax crayon. Age 13 years. Spatial deviation. Lower stream, secondary modern school

Another interesting example of spatial deviation was shown by a thirteen-year-old football fan, who persisted in making pictures with a sky between the football player and the spectators in the stands. He remained quite perplexed by his friends' criticism of this feature, even expressing genuine surprise because they did not know it that way.

Approximately one third of an E.S.N. class will find any real satisfaction from merely drawing and painting pictures, with a similar proportion at secondary school. However, there is still the tendency to regard these activities as the bases of all artistic expression from which one might judge the pupils' creativity. Quite often we are rather evaluating their ability or failure to translate the world of three-dimensional solids into a two-dimensional form. The problem invariably arises of the retarded pupil who becomes dissatisfied with his own meagre drawings, although often it will be possible to arouse enthusiasm if ideas are interpreted in some other medium.

If a child in making a drawing holds the pencil as though he were writing, the subsequent restriction of hand, wrist and arm movement will hardly be conducive to his making the freer lines and bolder form that one hopes to encourage, for it is only by using these that the pupil may begin to realize direction and rhythm that can be achieved in the lines he creates. The importance of working on a scale that is suitable for drawing with blackboard chalk, thick charcoal and crayon, rather than pencil, must be stressed, which with encouragement to make fuller use of hand, wrist and arm movements will wean a pupil from attempting niggling shape or detail.

Many spastics can hold crayons, but some downward pressure is also needed to make a bold line with these, which will not always be easy for the disabled who are confined to a wheel-chair. When a child uses a drawing material that will enable him to produce boldness of line without that effort, he can draw more freely and become aware of the rhythm or direction in his movements. The introduction of some unorthodox drawing material helps many mentally retarded pupils to work on such aspects when verbal encouragement would fail. The most effective art-teaching methods for many physically and mentally handicapped pupils are those in which some means for creativity can be established through physical experiences that they may learn to associate with achieving specific effects.

Salt

A child may learn to move his hand and fingers in a layer of salt which is spread before him over a dark surface so that the results of these movements will show. A working area of plyboard

Salt drawing. Age 10 years. Cerebral palsy, hemiplegic, without speech. Special school

Flour and water. Age 9 years. Cerebral palsy, hemiplegic. Special school

edged with flat picture-frame wood and painted black is most suitable.

At first it may be necessary to guide each hand gently through the salt until a child realizes some feeling of movement. This new sensation is enjoyed, but his own early attempts to repeat this invariably produce slight impressions on the surface, due to unused weak muscles or uncoordinated movements. One may observe other contributory factors, as in some cases of cerebral palsy, where the hand is held in an unnatural position or fingers remain clenched. It is then that one may gradually help to improve the hand position by rubbing the area above the wrist to reduce muscle tension so that a more relaxed and flattened hand may be guided to rotate the surface, taking care that the palm, fingers and sides are brought into use. Valuable exercises can become absorbing play activity in which the teacher is occasionally required to smooth the salt layer.

Quite soon the child can be asked to draw in the salt some familiar subject, such as a face or a man, thus expressing the image that he knows. Sometimes the results will reveal odd placing of features or scattered parts of the body, which might suggest some spatial difficulty.

Flour

Plain flour should be mixed with water to a thick cream and spread over part of a coloured background where it can be worked about to reveal areas of colour.

This method gives the child at an early stage of his art education some experience of clean, bright colour and opportunity to control its distribution with hand and finger movements. There will be no laborious cleaning to follow this activity as is necessary if finger paints are used for the same purpose.

Cut sheets of polythene (polyethylene) or coloured plastic for the background from bags made in bright opaque colours or, alternatively, use clear cooking film over coloured paper and stick it round the edges to a firm base with a plastic adhesive. These shiny surfaces are conducive to easy movements although the mixture is inclined to peel from them as it dries hard. Yet it will usually adhere sufficiently for the work to be displayed vertically for a couple of days before the flour mixture is brushed away to leave the background intact.

Seeds

Hand and finger movements may be attempted in a layer of seeds which have been spread over a background of expanded polystyrene.

Some kinds of seeds may be coloured artificially for this purpose, if they are put in a saucer of waterproof ink for an hour and then spread on blotting paper to dry. The introduction of coloured seeds against the white background will give clear results that may be stuck permanently in place with gum arabic or diluted PVA (polymer medium) trickled over the surface from a flexible bottle.

Plastic deodorant dispenser

Cut the base out with scissors and put in its place a cork or a cotton reel or spool that has been sawn across the middle. The

Age 11 years. Cerebral palsy, athetosis. Special school. The fish was made with grains of rice, dyed dark red. Lentils and unpolished rice were added afterwards

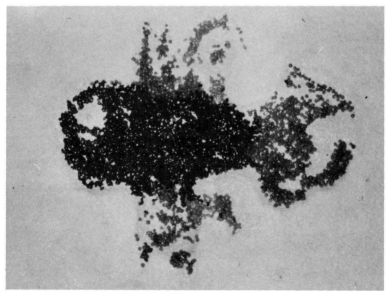

Plastic deodorant dispenser

Plastic slip tracer

ball end may be rolled over the drawing surface to leave behind an even trail of the liquid which it contains, or it may be used for filling in areas.

The container must be filled with a liquid that will flow easily yet be thick enough to control. Mix powder paints (powder tempera colour) with flour, starch, or PVA (polymer medium) or dilute water-based block printing colours with water.

Plastic slip tracer

Unscrew the nozzle so that the pliable plastic container can be half filled with the liquid described above. The slip tracer should be moved just above the drawing surface. The child squeezes the sides gently to release a thin liquid trail.

For drawing on cloth, the dispenser or slip tracer should be filled with fabric dye or ink that is mixed according to the thickness of line required. Thinning oil may be added to washable fabric ink, while fabric dye that can be thinned with water will require a warm iron passed over the cloth to fix it when it is dry.

'Lines'. Age 17 years. Cerebral palsy, hemiplegic. Special school. The lines were drawn on polystyrene with a deodorant dispenser

'Family group'. Age 11 years. Cerebral palsy, quadriplegic. Special school.
A first attempt with the deodorant dispenser

'The Sun'. Slip tracer drawing. Age 10 years. Cerebral palsy, without speech.
Special school

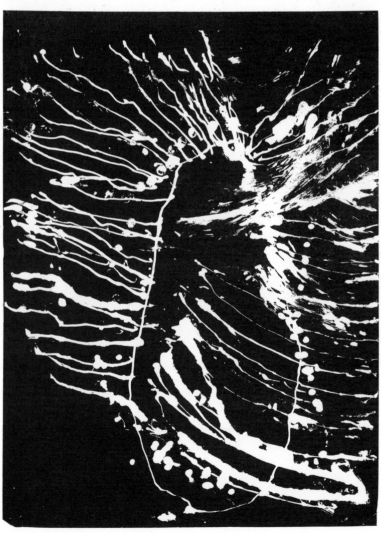

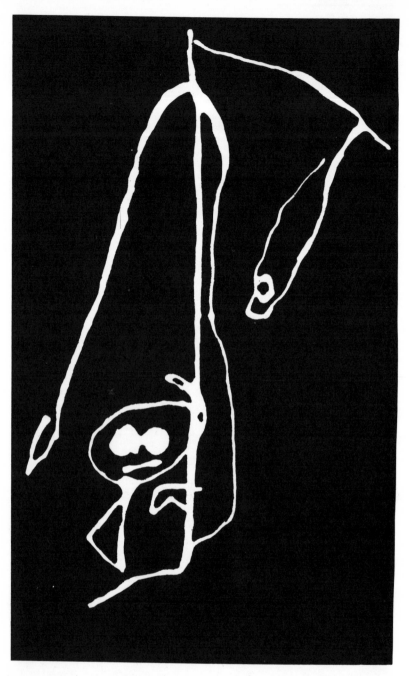

'Bell-ringing'. Age 11 years. Cerebral palsy, hemiplegic, without speech.
Slip tracer drawing by a boy who was learning bell-ringing. This was his first
means of communication with the outside world. Special school

If some plain-coloured shapes are printed on to the fabric first
with pieces broken from a polystyrene sheet, they will each
create a clearly defined area for drawing. Pleasing effects will be
obtained when the lines are added in black or a strongly contrasting colour.

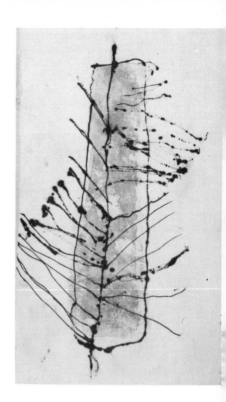

'Leaf'. Age 11 years. Cerebral palsy, quadriplegic. Special school. Section from a length of curtain material on which polystyrene shapes provided the basis for drawings of leaves

Headsquare. Age 11 years. Cerebral palsy, hemiplegic. Special school. Part of a design on tergal voile which combines drawing and printing. This boy extended an arm for the first time in his keenness to place overprints

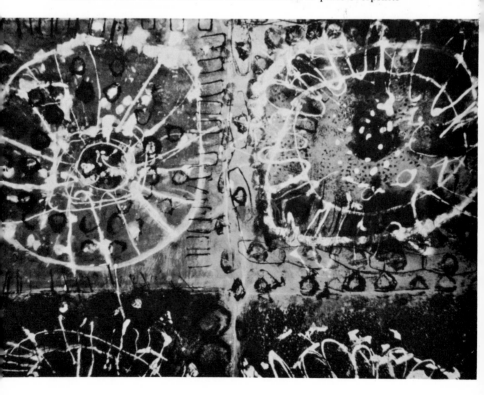

Bleach on brown sacking.
Age 15 years. Cerebral palsy,
hemiplegic. Special school

Print from cold solder on fine
copper gauze. Age 11 years.
Cerebral palsy, quadriplegic.
Special school

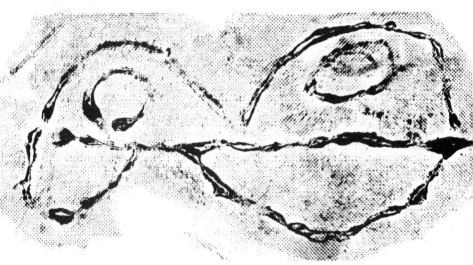

Bleach

When liquid bleach is used for drawing on coloured fabric it removes the colour beneath so that all lines and spots which are made will show in effective contrast to the background. Particularly clear results are obtained when coloured hessian (sacking) or home dyed cotton is used.

One very small pliable plastic bottle will be required about three-quarters full of household bleach. Push a strip of foam rubber into it so that it touches the bottom and protrudes half an inch at the top. Liquid will be emitted as this foam rubber touches the fabric, while an increased flow will be obtained by gently squeezing the bottle. Bleaching takes place within a short time, then the fabric is rinsed in water.

Solder and glue

Cold liquid solder or plastic glue may be squeezed directly from the tube to draw raised lines and textural effects. These can often be printed, or added to create contrasts in work where paint, Polyfilla (Spackle) and polish are used.

Slip

Drawings may be used to decorate tiles if you have access to a kiln. Make the tiles by rolling clay on a board with a rolling-pin and then cutting round a wood template. The drawing itself is made with slip – clay that has been mixed with water to a creamy consistency and passed through a sieve. Fill the tracer with a slip that contrasts in colour with that of the tiles which should be still damp when the slip is applied. It is important to use clays for both tiles and slip which will contract equally when they are fired.

Clay tile. Age 12 years. E.S.N. Special school

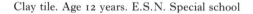

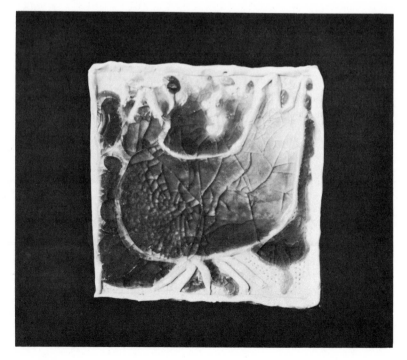

Polyfilla (Spackle)

Alternatively, when a kiln is not available, glass-smooth tiles can be made from dental plaster, Polyfilla or Spackle. Work an inch-thick roll of plasticine round a small sheet of glass made wet to ensure a satisfactory bond. Mix the powder according to the instructions, pour it on to the glass and leave it to set. Once hard the plasticine can be removed and the tile slid from the base.

A coloured trail can be made on the tile with the slip tracer if powder colour is added to the plaster mixture. The 'instant' variety of Polyfilla can be used direct from the tube if it is manipulated well before it is handed to the child. Care must be taken to touch the tile's surface as drawing proceeds, otherwise this trail may remain in a cylindrical roll and fail to adhere.

Plaster

Intaglio drawings may be made on a plaster tile, using fine points and lino gouges to obtain a variety of line. If the surface is painted black, the child will be able to see his progress as he goes along. He may then ink the tile with a rubber roller and take a print from it by laying a sheet of paper over the top and rotating a pad of tissue paper over the back. A black and white print will accentuate the line variation and help to arouse a pupil's interest.

Wax crayon

Alternatively drawings can be scratched on a surface that is made by rubbing white and then black wax crayon over white card (see drawing page 50).

Aluminium foil

Attractive wall plaques in relief can be made after transferring a simple outline pencil drawing on to a sheet of aluminium foil spread underneath it. An empty ball-point pen should be used to draw over the original outlines, and the result will immediately be enhanced as it appears slightly raised on the reverse side of the foil. The idea may then be developed freely by filling in areas with dots, lines and cross-hatching, to create textural effects. Pliers with smooth curved handles are useful for rubbing gently across surfaces, either to obliterate errors or to press back some parts so as to produce greater relief in others.

Aluminium foil. Age 11 years. Lowest stream, secondary modern school

Electric sewing-machine

Some pupils are able to draw by stitching with an electric sewing-machine. They use the stitch regulator to reverse direction, and make curves by gently moving the fabric while the needle is in motion.

Spastics practise with the speed controller worked slowly for them so that they can feel the direction of the lines that are made and learn to associate these with certain actions on their part. When this has been established, they may work the speed controller for themselves. It might involve using a foot which has to be lifted into position with their hands. If this is the case, a

Pattern disk for electric sewing-machine

Fabric dye on organdie. Age 11 years.
Cerebral palsy, ataxia. Special school

Age 14 years. Appliqué and machine
stitching in silver lurex and Sylko
synthetic thread. Sequins are glued
into place. The work of a girl with
congenital deformities. She has
malformation of both shoulders and
arms reaching only to the elbows,
with small fingers attached. There is
movement in the fingers, but the
thumbs are useless. Special school

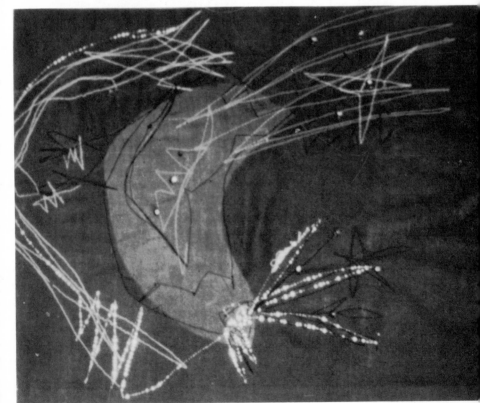

Age 16 years. Cerebral palsy, hemiplegic. Special school. Polystyrene print and machine stitching with the speed controller pressed by foot, despite surgical boots

Machine stitching. Age 12 years. Cerebral palsy, ataxia. Special school. This result was achieved by working the speed controller with finger pressure

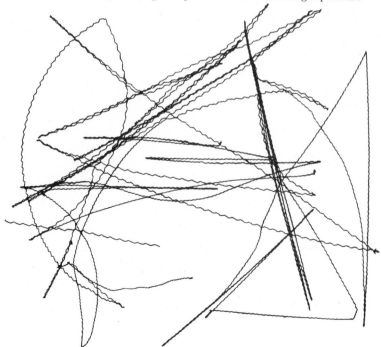

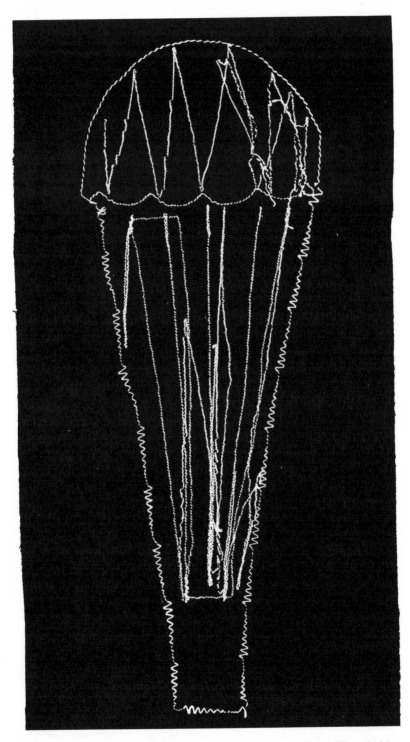

'Parachute'. Age 14 years. Cerebral palsy, ataxia. Special school. The stitching
is worked on black Vilene (Pellon) and shows the use of embroidery disks

heavy weight must be provided to keep the control unit in place. Alternatively, a knee lever can be used or the speed controller placed on a chair at the side and worked by finger pressure.

Stitching is done from one reel of Sylko (synthetic thread) that will show effectively against the background. A firm fabric such as felt or Vilene (Pellon) will prove the most manageable, particularly when only one hand is able to control it. Any rucking can then be prevented by gently pulling a corner of fabric as it leaves the machine.

Looseness of line can be achieved by combining machine-stitching with a simple shape printed on fabric. Suitable shapes can also be made by blowing on to blobs of fabric dye through a firm plastic drinking straw.

Some who have cerebral palsy are able to press pattern disks in position on the sewing-machine and use these freely in working their creations, changing from patterns to ordinary stitching while keeping a continuous thread. Many of these pupils eventually learn to synchronize their movements with the machine so successfully that they are then able to follow definite outlines.

Painting

Pupils should always find pots of paint already mixed and ready to use. At training centre level results will generally show colours daubed on paper without purposeful intent, although there may also be indications that some have obviously found pleasure through the physical movement experienced when working in particular directions.

One mongol girl I knew would paint at an easel, making bold up and down strokes with the long-handled brush held firmly at the top and absorbed in feeling the full action involved. Among an older group, a fifteen-year-old autistic girl painted her colours with definite circular movements. She also liked to use the hand sewing-machine, making small bags by machining straight lines to join the sides, although this was primarily for the pleasure which the motion of turning the handle and seeing the wheel rotate afforded her.

I have already pointed out that autistic children become obsessed at various times by certain things such as lights, straight lines or a particular colour. It is important to introduce creative activities which follow their obsessions in order to try and induce some purposeful response from these pupils. An autistic girl would stand fascinated by a row of tall trees which could be seen outside the window. When a straight line was drawn for her during this phase, she would eagerly dash down her copy beside it in paint and the procedure could be repeated many times.

It is often noticeable that by secondary school stage quite a number of pupils persist in making what they term 'pattern'. This is a defence barrier, for they hope it will hide their inability to be creative. Such lack of confidence can only be dispelled by introducing an entirely different creative activity or a new approach to painting, where the nature of the material itself will provoke their interest. There are pupils too in all groups, who will repeat a past success rather than create a new idea, until what was originally self-expression becomes a symbol of their mental stagnation and should be discouraged. It is of course a special trait in those who have autistic tendencies, so that one girl who always painted a particular group of flowers was eventually warned that if she persisted, her paper would be removed. This had actually to be done several times in succession before she started to draw a house and introduced the flowers beside it. The sequence had been broken and from that time she continued to produce other ideas.

Sponge

A pupil may realize direction more readily through the move-

Age 12 years. Cerebral palsy, hemiplegic. Special school. Shows the results of free sweeping movements made with a sponge on white painted plywood. Light blue shoe polish is combined with black, bright green and deep yellow powder tempera colour in which texture appears where paint overlaps the polish

ments he makes if he is given a sponge instead of a brush for painting.

A portion of synthetic sponge yields to the weakest or most unorthodox grip while offering no resistance to any substance, so that through holding such pliable material one may be sensitive to the surface beneath.

This makes it useful to the child who is unable to hold a paint brush or for one who has spatial difficulties and must rely on feeling the boundaries of areas to be coloured. Synthetic sponge may therefore be used for applying paint to some of the modelled work, and it is also ideal for attempting free movements on paper after it has been dipped in powder colour or rubbed across coloured shoe polish.

Painting materials can be difficult to organize for the badly handicapped wheel-chair pupil, but a useful palette is made by covering a wooden board with sheet foam rubber. Mix paints to the consistency of thick cream and apply them to the foam rubber in saturated areas. Spread coloured shoe polish liberally on other parts of its surface. Fix sponges above each colour by pushing them between two large nails. They should be returned here immediately after use. This palette may be clamped at any

'Direction'. Painting with brush and palette knife. Age 12 years. Lowest stream, secondary modern school

convenient angle without the contents spilling and only occasional replenishing is needed.

The palette knife

It is sometimes possible to increase the sensory experience of some mentally handicapped pupils through painting by giving them polymer water-based emulsion paints that can be applied with a palette knife. Exciting textural effects may be obtained by laying colour on thickly or simply varying the direction of palette knife strokes.

This method may also be used to help others release pent up feelings of aggression which might otherwise lead to violent outbursts. Such anti-social energies directed towards the making of violent strokes and colours in a child's creative activity help to relieve the tension within. There is much truth in the expression 'seeing red' as a descriptive term for anger, but an opportunity to translate this literally into action painting can prove much safer for those around, particularly if violence is the outcome of an epileptic condition, when even a pupil of small stature may display maniac strength. Similarly, the potential fire-raiser through his paintings of burning buildings created

'Bang!' Polymer emulsion and palette knife. Age 12 years. Lowest stream, secondary modern school

by this method will be helped towards developing more socially acceptable behaviour.

One must remember that some emotionally disturbed children are only too painfully aware of their uncontrolled behaviour and without reprimand will immediately become bitterly ashamed of themselves after each violent outburst, only to fail again. Their need is to realize an inner calm through absorbing occupation so that they may gradually establish a pattern of orderly progression in life. When strong emotion can be harnessed to suitable creative movement, it is less easily aroused in a negative way.

The choice of subject can be important in palette-knife

painting and one which can be mimed with a few simple actions will prove most suitable, as pupils may then follow the main direction of these movements with their palette knife strokes and so learn to associate their own body movements with the creation of line. They might illustrate in this way the bending of trees in the teeth of a gale; waves dashing against rocks; the opposing impact of demonstrators; or the outward thrust in an explosion. Further emphasis can be added by dragging a brush handle through the polymer emulsion or scratching surfaces. There would seem little doubt that its plasticity can encourage many who find it difficult to control a fluid mixture to experiment with form and colour.

The brush

The E.S.N. child can often be more painfully aware of his inadequacies than is generally realized. Consequently, if he is to become interested in painting pictures with a brush there must be some assurance of his having reasonable success. This can in some cases be given by reducing the pitfalls of picture-making to a minimum.

Mix paint to the consistency of thick cream and put it out ready for use in jars. Colours should have as wide a range as possible, and might contain pink, orange, turquoise or purple paint, dark and light primary colours with white also. Violet or dark blue should be used instead of black, which is so intense that it can easily permeate the whole colour range through the slightest carelessness, reducing it to drabness and subsequently ruining the work. It is important that good standards of colour should be introduced and intermixing kept to a minimum so that the pupil may be helped in maintaining those standards. I stress the value at junior school stage of pupils learning to control good clean colour provided as opposed to intermixing colours freely, the miserable consequences of which are all too obvious even in the reception classes of secondary selective schools. Discrimination of colour and tone values is a gradual process which complete licence does not help the majority to achieve.

Give the child charcoal or chalk to indicate, very simply, an area on the paper which the subject of his picture will occupy, and get him to make some attempt at basic shapes. Set a straightforward problem in composition which may be solved quite easily, rather than a multiple suggestion or a scene, which is too complex. A single subject theme such as a portrait, or a simple two-part composition of perhaps the 'cat on the mat' is best. The

'Fantasy'. Age 13 years. E.S.N. Special school

discipline of planning first in even rudimentary form is important and impulsive starts should be discouraged.

A bold statement of ideas must be encouraged throughout, so the main part of the picture will be painted with a large long-handled brush. The size of paper must be big enough to allow for adequate hand movement in manipulating the brush. Furthermore, a thinner brush that is useful for putting in the small detail should not be produced until towards the end of the lesson. There can then be no temptation to complete one section of the picture too early, so that it remains unrelated to the rest.

'Contrasts'. Age 14 years. Special school. Illustrating make-up applied to half the face only, as a means for introducing E.S.N. girls to the use of contrast in design. Later, similar faces were cut in lino and printed on fabric

Fantasy subjects are popular because the pupil can have an entirely free choice of colours and there can be no failure on his part to conform to reality. Monsters, clowns, magic birds, flowers or bicycles, pirates and Red Indians, are all illustrated from the world of make-believe. The fifteen- to sixteen-year-old group will also like a colourful still life which they can rearrange on paper and paint in their own choice of colours if they wish. E.S.N. pupils also enjoy illustrating certain occupations, particularly if these represent roles in which they see themselves. Popular figures are the footballer, soldier, sailor, airman, nurse, bride, and mother with perambulator. It would never occur to the layman looking at a display of all these gay, bold paintings, that many are simply an expression of escapism; yet through being helped to discover satisfaction in creative expression, many handicapped children may feel a sense of achievement, which in itself will help to restore their self-respect.

More than a choice of suitable topics is often needed to retain the pupils' interest in painting and it may be possible to do this through extending their colour experience.

'Ambition'. Age 12 years. E.S.N. Special school

'Ambition'. Age 13 years. E.S.N.
Special school

Circus mural for assembly hall.
Special school incorporating E.S.N.
and handicapped sections. Polystyrene coated with Polyfilla
(Spackle). Ideas worked out in-
dividually with torn paper and paint,
then arranged on the background for
the main outlines to be drawn and
painted with polymer colours

This is achieved by actually restricting them to a limited range of colour. Pictures should be painted either with the red–orange–yellow or blue–green–yellow range of the colour spectrum. Intermixing with violet and white paint should be encouraged. Some pupils will derive satisfaction in painting predominantly with red, blue or green by experimenting further in mixing tones of colour.

Topics for illustration might then be attempted that will depend upon the creation of simple shapes and tone contrasts to produce dramatic effects. Aircraft flying at sunset, or the stark remains of cars and lorries in a scrapyard might be suitable themes, or even a football poster bearing the name of a favourite team. It is when the subject content or a method of using colour makes an emotional appeal to a pupil that painting may help him in coming to terms with his own feelings and situation.

One emotionally disturbed boy, aged twelve years, who attended secondary modern school, would devise different techniques of using paint to satisfy his moods. At one period, he painted subjects in which all shapes were composed of

'Scrapyard'. Age 11 years. Secondary modern school, lower stream

Technique influenced by mood. Age 12 years. Emotionally disturbed.
Secondary modern school, lowest stream

innumerable multi-coloured blobs which he would stab or
grind into place. Gradually this technique became less violent,
because, like the Pointillists at the close of the last century, he
became absorbed in the colour effects which could be obtained
in this way, when the colours of these blobs or spots placed close
together are blended by vision and not the brush.

Modelling

In order to create form out of the plastic substance of any modelling material, reasonable manual control is needed together with some idea of solid shape. It is therefore not very surprising to find that this can be impossible where a child is limited in both these experiences. No pupil can really begin to appreciate the creation of simple form until he has actually handled it. This is why suitable shapes are sometimes introduced as moulds for building round with papier-mâché, for they must then be manipulated constantly.

Clay may be very satisfying to manipulate, but its plasticity offers little clue to its limitations, while a certain degree of manual dexterity is also needed before it can be modelled with any success. The usual ill-defined shapes with the scattered appendages that will be shed as they dry, are typical of even normal child effort and result from fashioning small pieces of clay with fingers only. This may be overcome to some extent by

Clay head. Age 11 years. Secondary modern school, lowest stream

encouraging pupils to model large lumps of clay which will require the use of both hands. They might then become more aware of the three-dimensional quality of the clay and shape all parts accordingly. Here, however, it must still be assumed that pupils have some concept of form, for without it there can be no particular merit in using clay as modelling material.

Processes that require direct contact with plastic materials provide an outlet for feelings of frustration or aggression and are often suitable for some emotionally disturbed pupils. It is noticeable, however, that autistic children dislike making themselves dirty and find it impossible to become involved in any release of emotional energy by this means.

There are many useful modelling techniques based upon the versatility of paper, which many handicapped pupils can successfully perform. These involve valuable hand and finger

Using shapes. Age 10 years. Cerebral palsy, hemiplegic. Special school. Impressed design with finger or found objects. Buttons and bottle tops may also be pressed into the surface to remain there

'Sleeping figure'. Age 14 years. Cerebral palsy, hemiplegic. Special school. This girl was so severely handicapped that only two fingers could be used to model the plasticine

movements by which work can be produced in relief. Such activity will therefore commend itself to the needs of the blind and partially sighted.

Using shapes

Although it may be possible for a spastic to use both hands, any process which will involve their simultaneous action often proves difficult because of his uncoordinated movements.

When a child tries to press a mixture of papier-mâché and Polyfilla (Spackle) round a plastic bottle or flower-pot made of expanded polystyrene, he may display an inability to exert manual pressure on the shape. This might improve with practice if some time has been spent in guiding the hands through the process and gently exerting the required pressure over them. It is then that the child may actually feel the shape and in this way acquire a knowledge of simple form.

Plasticine

Attempts at rolling pieces of plasticine into lengths or balls can provide a valuable flattening exercise for the fingers and palm. Plasticine does not need continual attention to keep it in a workable condition and spastics seem to find it easier to handle than clay. The fact that it has a tendency to become very soft with constant handling is no disadvantage here.

If a damp sheet of perspex (acrylic) or metal is used as a base, the child can press rolled plasticine pieces to anchor firmly on it and sometimes add others to make a small figure.

Papier-mâché and Polyfilla (Spackle). Age 16 years. Cerebral palsy, hemiplegic. Special school

Polyfilla (Spackle). Age 12 years. Cerebral palsy, hemiplegic. Special school

Papier-mâché and Polyfilla (Spackle)

Sometimes a pupil will show a tendency to grip things too fiercely and for this he can be helped with the finger movement involved in tearing newspaper into pieces to make papier-mâché. If the newspaper has previously been left to soak in water for at least twelve hours, he will have practice in adjusting his touch to make the light and small movements required for tearing it.

He can then hand mix the pulped papier-mâché with Polyfilla or Spackle, cellulose fillers which set at a slower rate than plaster of Paris and can be mixed to the consistency of thick cream. In this the hand becomes more relaxed as it continually grasps, squeezes and scoops through the soft mixture, with movements consequently becoming more controlled. He may then spread a thick layer over an expanded polystyrene sheet. The same grasping and smoothing movements can produce interesting effects in relief that will be made permanent if left to dry for a few days.

Once this has been mastered a stiff mixture of cellulose filler only may be used, which will set within an hour. Hand and finger movements must become adjusted to this different consistency before definite contours can be created.

Newspaper

Simple modelling in relief may be attempted with several layers of paste-sodden newspaper.

The work can be carried out on a background of cardboard or expanded polystyrene over which is laid a double sheet of newspaper, which should be larger than the background. The side uppermost should be pasted liberally with a hand that has been dipped in a bowl of cellulose paste. Another similar sheet of newspaper should be laid over the first, but it does not have to be placed accurately. The process should be repeated until four layers of well-pasted newspaper are stuck together.

Newspaper. Age 13 years. Cerebral palsy, ataxia. Special school

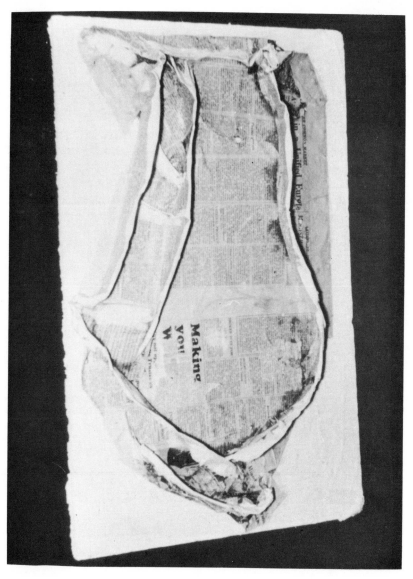

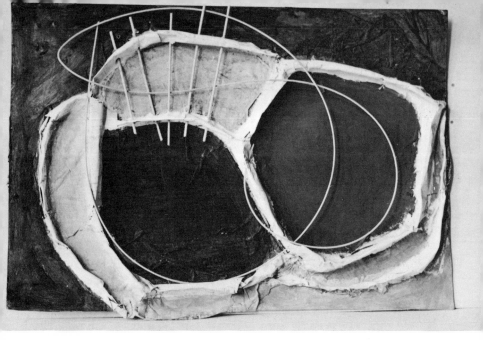

Moulded newspaper sheets. Age 11 years. Secondary modern school, lowest stream

This saturated material can be modelled with the hands into ridges or mounds, and not only will it adhere to the background already in position underneath, but any surplus newspaper may finally be folded to stick at the back.

Abstract designs made in this way will provide tangible evidence for many E.S.N. and backward pupils that a satisfactory creation depends upon achieving some relationship between material and background.

The newspaper sheets pasted together as one unit to be contained within the bounds of a smaller background, make it necessary for pupils to consider this as a dominant shape. They will never regard a background as such until confronted with this actual physical problem. The creation of several shapes modelled from one unit means that some unity in design is inevitable, whereas the more usual collage methods that are used for this purpose involve the arranging of separate units and do not direct the child's attention to this aspect.

Modelled shapes provide the bases for other creative activities, as many handicapped pupils will be guided by these when colouring or arranging various other materials.

Tarlatan

Pasted tarlatan fabric of single thickness may be moulded more delicately than newspaper. Although it demands finer finger movements, this thin material will not become unwieldy if the cellulose paste is spread over it after it has been placed on the dry background.

Moulded newspaper strips. Age 12 years. Secondary modern school, lowest stream

Newspaper strips

Pasted newspaper strips can be moulded into shape with the fingers and it is possible to use them for three-dimensional work.

A head can be made on a cardboard carton base that is packed tightly with crumpled paper. Features can be added with firm ridges of newspaper. These should be made of several strips stuck together, each approximately three inches in width, which will be folded and pasted again before moulding them to the background.

Cartridge paper (white drawing paper)

Strips of cartridge paper, approximately one inch wide, may be used for creating outlines in relief.

Each strip should be folded down the middle and cuts should be made with scissors at intervals along one side of it. It is then possible to bend the strips to the required shape before sticking them on the background by means of the fringed pieces.

Folded paper. Age 11 years. Secondary modern school pupil recently recovered from a fractured skull

Patterned paper bags. Age 12 years. Cerebral palsy, hemiplegic. Special school

Corrugated cardboard and threads. Age 10 years. E.S.N. Special school

Paper bags

Shape can be created out of a thin paper bag by putting the hand inside and pressing part of it on to a cardboard or expanded polystyrene background which has been covered with a layer of cellulose paste.

The bag can be stuffed loosely with tissue paper or twisted, creased and pinched into shape with fingers that have been dipped in paste. Light materials such as drinking straws may be added. Interesting results are achieved by using striped and patterned bags of different sizes.

Corrugated cardboard

Large beads can be made from corrugated cardboard that has been cut into long tapering strips. The shape and length of each bead will be determined largely by the width of the tapered end. Each strip should be rolled firmly round a length of round wood dowel rod, commencing at the untapered end. This end should then be fixed with PVA adhesive.

Beads may be threaded on wire and dipped in varnish or paint. Alternatively, they may be coated with adhesive before winding on fine threads and lurex used directly from the spool. The finished beads may be strung on thick cords or wires which, if attached to a length of dowel rod, will make a wall hanging.

Carving

Many handicapped pupils will derive great satisfaction from activity which involves cutting into surfaces. Whether this develops into the creation of three-dimensional form depends as much upon the materials as on the direction and boldness of movements used.

Brick, balsa and 'Thermalite' (fibreglass)

Although brick or balsa block is quite easily carved with a file, the limitations imposed by its size with the precision of surface and form, will make such material hardly conducive to creating freer shape in three dimensions. Even the larger fibreglass building-block called 'Thermalite', that is also easy to file into shape, does not inspire the creation of different form as will

Carving in brick. Age 11 years. Secondary modern school, lowest stream

Age 12 years. Secondary modern school, lowest stream. This boy carved a pattern with his door key on a small piece of Thermalite he had found on his way to school. It was by bringing it to paint during an art lesson that his interest in fabric printing began

Age 12 years. Emotionally disturbed. Secondary modern school. A first attempt at carving a head from a lump of Thermalite, which was then printed

happen when a large, irregular chunk is used. Surface cutting can also lead to experimental printing activities and the carving of simple relief.

Shapes which are large and heavy enough to be free standing will make it easier for both physically and mentally handicapped pupils to concentrate on the actual carving processes.

Natural chalk

Chunks of natural chalk are suitable for creating work in three dimensions particularly because they can provide interesting irregular shapes.

Dental plaster

Dental plaster makes an excellent substitute for chalk. Half fill a bowl with cold water and sprinkle some dental plaster evenly across the surface. Most of it will sink to the bottom. Continue doing this until the plaster rises to the surface, and when all bubbling has ceased, hold the hand horizontally with palm downwards, and rapidly agitate the mixture beneath the

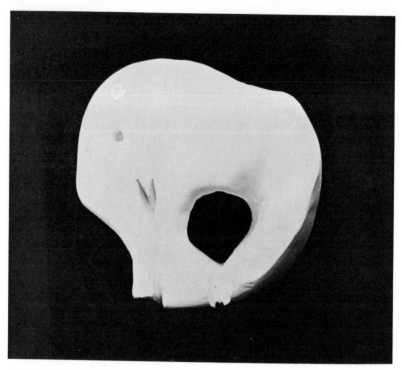

Carving in dental plaster. Age 15 years. E.S.N. Special school

surface until no sediment remains. The mixture can then be poured into strong plastic bags or cardboard boxes to set. Use clothes pegs, office spring clips, string or wire to distort the shapes of the containers before pouring in the mixture.

Irregularity in the shape of block that is used is important, for it will provide immediate objectives for using rasps or surform tools and can often be developed by filing areas away, learning to smooth others, or boring channels right through. Irregular shape can stir the imagination, suggesting the form which the work will take, whether abstract or representational. It will also encourage those who find difficulty in committing themselves to any deliberate action, especially since the tools used will make this a very gradual process. Such activity can help many to gain self-confidence and often proves suitable for those with slow mental powers, who are likely to spoil their material when using more direct methods of carving. Others are able to work out aggression or frustration through a command of tools and material, especially if they are creating something fairly large. At the same time the rhythmical sound of the filing, coupled with the emergence of shapes which are created, can have a salutary effect.

Since the work will entail the continuous smoothing of all surfaces with fine sandpaper and the development of holes and curves from all directions, the pupils begin to realize how separate parts can become integrated. The need for simple curves and the avoidance of sharp projections will be appreciated

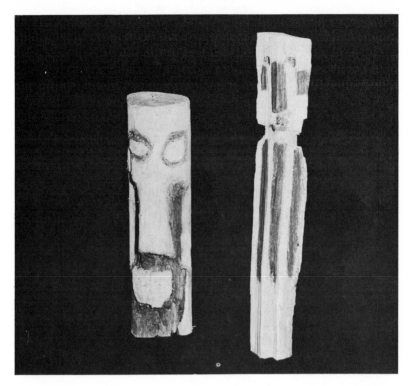

Carving in wood. Age 12 years. Lowest stream, secondary modern school

through practical experience as they polish the finished carving by rubbing a candle over the surface and polishing gently with a soft cloth. A highly-polished brightly-coloured finish may be obtained in the same way, if prepared household dye has previously been poured over the plaster. It is in their desire to obtain these effects that children will eagerly attempt all possible simplification. The repetitive nature of the various processes involved in the production of one piece of work will also provide them with opportunities for practising valuable hand or finger movement which may gradually be improved by practical suggestion from the teacher.

Wood

Driftwood or portions of dead branches often have interesting shapes and make suitable carving material for some E.S.N. pupils. The wood should be fixed in a vice so that the child has both hands free to control the knives and chisels.

Placing

Activities involving the placing of various materials, which may appear physically possible for a handicapped pupil to perform, will often prove difficult for him to carry out. This is because the limitations of a straightforward congenital deformity might be obvious, but when the more elusive handicaps such as visuo-motor or perceptual disorders intervene, these can cause hitherto unsuspected obstacles as a pupil tries to place his material, and will often prove formidable barriers to the acquirement of knowledge.

In his first years at school the normal child has already acquired much practical experience concerning the nature of things as he moves freely about his environment. He is even beginning to compare and classify his experiences, besides developing more realistic concepts of size, weight, space and distance. It is therefore important to ensure that the handicapped child has opportunities not only for handling a wealth of material, but also to manipulate this through creative activity and so increase his knowledge in these directions.

An inability to copy a formation of coloured bricks or sticks does not necessarily show that a child cannot perceive the relevant clues before him, such as differences and similarities in size, shape or colour. This could rather be an indication of visuo-motor disorder when a defective co-ordination between hand and eye makes it difficult for him to manipulate spatial relationships, often despite the possession of some perceptual acuity.

Many cerebral palsied and other brain-damaged children will therefore be helped in placing their materials through the introduction of subtle aids of a non-visual kind. These will take the form of physical boundaries to surround the area of creative activity and may be provided by using shallow frames or moulds that are actually incorporated as part of a design, where they will clearly define areas for placing the materials. It is by feeling the edges of these that many handicapped children are able to realize the relative position of their units and so place them more accurately. Sometimes these children may even learn to mould boundaries for themselves.

Some, as they press objects into firmly fixed blocks of polystyrene, will be guided by feeling the shape of the object as they proceed. Where it is possible, opportunities should also be given for making simple constructions. Pieces of polystyrene sheet and block sections from packaging in the same material can be joined upwards and outwards by means of cocktail sticks pushed into their surface. All these activities will enable many who have spatial difficulties to realize the position of their

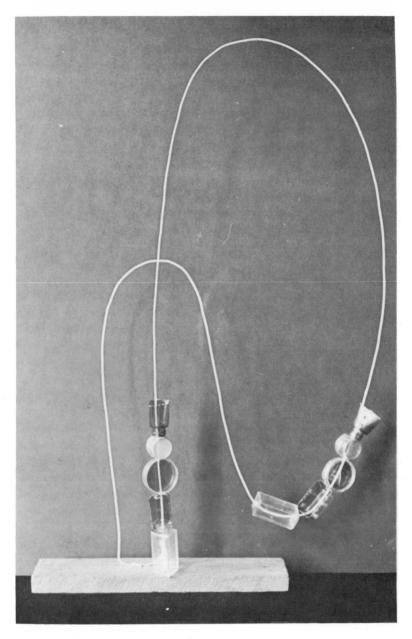

'Switchback' apparatus for placing shapes

own body to the units that they are placing. At least some of the confusion associated with manipulation may often be clarified by helping children to acquire even limited sensory motor experiences through creative activity that will also improve the kinaesthetic sensation.

The spatial ability of autistic children may be relatively intact and often much better developed than the level of performance might suggest. They have difficulty, however, in imitating, which alone would prevent them from placing material in any set pattern.

In an attempt to simplify the placing and matching of shapes for S.S.N. autistic children in one special school, a vertical switchback was made from galvanized iron wire, on which five pairs of acetate shapes were strung, each pair being a different shape. Although it was possible to pick out three pairs according to whether they were yellow, scarlet or clear acetate, two pairs could not be identified in this way, as they were both blue.

The idea of a switchback was decided upon after seeing several autistic children engrossed in watching sand or water which they trickled down from above the head. Acetate was used in preference to other material, so that they could see the light shining through, as some of these children had become obsessed by the shafts of light that fell on shiny and translucent surfaces. It was felt necessary to include these features in order that the apparatus might attract their attention. It was significant that they had not shown the slightest interest in a manufactured toy made from similar material but consisting of separate units, because perceptual defects prevented them from manipulating these in any meaningful way. The apparatus was then placed in a prominent position for the children to play with, when their performance could be observed.

It was interesting to watch the way some examined the apparatus, often seeming at first to look beyond it, then glancing quickly and turning away. A child using peripheral vision will do this and give the impression of being completely uninterested in the whole affair, if it were not for the fact that he still remains sitting there of his own free will! The manipulation of shapes on the switchback was controlled for the pupils to some extent, as they could push these only upwards or downwards along the wire. Several children concerned themselves only with the movement that this involved.

One girl, aged nine, spent some time doing this and each time she heard the clicking sound of a shape as it fell to the wooden base, would look either in her lap or towards the floor. After twenty minutes she had actually moved the shapes round so that they were exactly paired on two parallel wires. She then moved these on the switchback and paired the shapes again, but in a different order. This pupil had obviously realized the similarity of shape, as on both occasions immediately after pairing the shapes she was seen to be carefully examining each pair with her fingers.

Sometimes autistic children will thread beads on strings or wire, for it does seem that there are many of these children who may be helped to realize some sense of order if they are presented with activities which restrict their field of movement. One can appreciate from this the problem of an intelligent autistic girl, aged ten, who could use a paint brush quite well but with a collage immediately became confused because it involved an ability to organize and control the various units such as paste, brush, scissors and various pieces of material.

An ability to distinguish colours is usually fostered in the autistic child as this will provide him with a useful basis on which other learning processes may be developed and which could lead to a wide range of activities. Many autistic children are often helped to discern form, shape or colour by a sense other than sight, perhaps using materials of different textures. Alternatively, since some will be seen to distinguish objects by licking or smelling, certain smells such as lavender, cloves or onion can be rubbed into fabric so that these pupils may associate the relevant information with them. Eventually they may continue to identify their material even when such sensory clues have been withdrawn.

When the need for sensory experience is so vital, and frequently in non-visual ways, why is it that the conventional jigsaw puzzle still often remains as an activity for many physically and mentally handicapped pupils, both at junior training and special schools? Success in putting a puzzle together is dependent upon the child's ability to recognize a similarity between complicated and often indistinct shapes and spaces, with additional clues from the portion of printing or colour on each piece. While all these clues are invariably so indefinite as to require the utmost scrutiny in an attempt to reconstruct some adult illustration, such puzzles are frequently presented where normal powers of observation are often minimal! An activity will be of little value to many handicapped pupils until their sensory responses have been enhanced in more tangible ways.

Suitable puzzles for some mentally handicapped children might prove to be a box of round, cylindrical and egg shapes in different sizes, that are painted white, and which can be pulled apart or completed. It is comparatively easy nowadays to make an interesting collection of these simple shapes from plastic or cardboard packaging. The constant manipulation that such puzzles involve will help a child to gain some idea of shape and dimension.

Select suitable units from discarded man-made and natural materials, and provide each of them in quantity so that areas can be filled with identical shapes to make mosaics or textured panels. Some materials may be arranged in a layer of Polyfilla (Spackle) so that they become permanently fixed as it dries, while others such as hairpins, nails and matchsticks may simply be pushed into polystyrene.

Metal frame

A child may learn to arrange his materials within well-defined outlines, which will help him in placing them. This possibility of feeling the outlines will be of more use than any visual aid, particularly if the child has spatial difficulties or defective vision. A found object, such as the metal frame of an old wheel, fixed to the working surface is excellent for this purpose.

Age 12 years. Cerebral palsy, hemiplegic. Special school. Textural effects using drinking straws, broken household tiles, cotton reels, spools, matchboxes, shells, pegs, seeds and metal rings

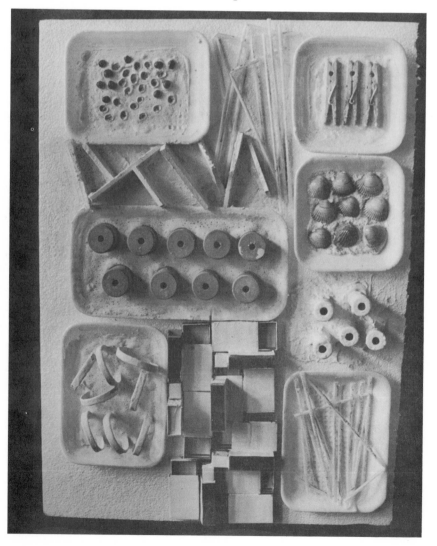

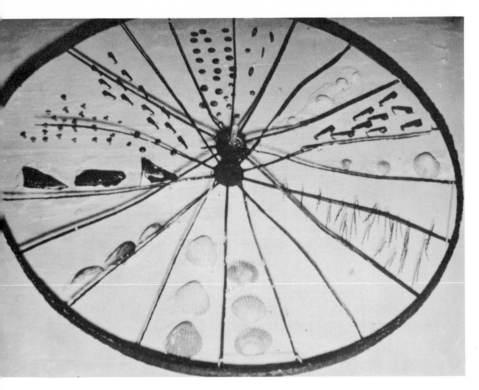

Inside a wheel. Age 11 years. Cerebral palsy, ataxia. Special school

'Castle'. Age 12 years. Cerebral palsy, athetosis, without speech. Special school. Household tiles, including broken pieces, arranged in a thin layer of Polyfilla (Spackle) so that they touch. Paint applied with a sponge

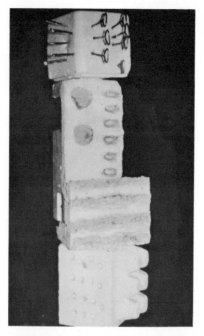

Polystyrene blocks. Age 13 years. Cerebral palsy, hemiplegia. Special school. Found objects were added to the blocks and an acorn twisted into the surface to make impressions. Long metal hairpins were pushed through the blocks to hold them together

Pliable shapes. Age 9 years. Junior school, lower stream

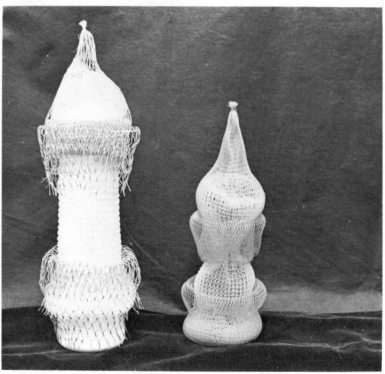

Food containers

Shallow disposable polystyrene food containers of different sizes may be dipped in thick Polyfilla (Spackle) to fix them on a sheet of polystyrene. They should be arranged against each other with some spaces deliberately left to show areas of back-

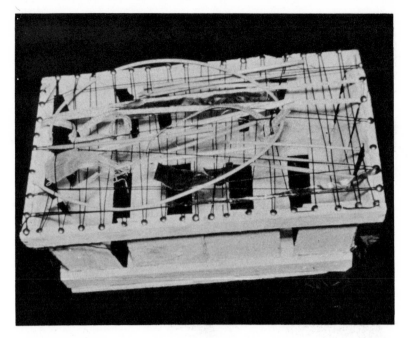

Working on strings. Age 16 years. Cerebral palsy, hemiplegic. Special school

ground. Textural effects are created by placing the various materials in parts of this arrangement.

Net bags, plastic bottles and round boxes

Some handicapped children find difficulty in dressing themselves, not only because of uncoordinated movement, but through an inability to deduce a relationship between their own body and the way into the garment. The 'clumsy' child may be helped by activity in which he can practise placing flimsy shapes over three-dimensional form.

A selection of pliable shapes can be obtained by using the small coloured nylon net bags in which fruit, vegetables or horticultural products are sometimes purchased. Nylon and metal pot scourers can also be pulled out into long shaped bags. A collection of plastic bottles and round boxes is also needed.

The nylon bags can be stretched over the bottles and boxes, pulled over each other, or folded back to create different shapes, textures and colour effects. Imaginary towers and kiosks can be created in this way.

Wooden vegetable box

Some pupils with physical handicap or brain dysfunction will find it easier to work in a vertical direction and any inducement to direct and extend movements about the whole spatial field is an essential therapy for many.

An upright work frame can be made from a wooden vegetable

box which will stand firmly on its side. When upholstery nails with large heads are fixed evenly along the four top edges of this the child is able to wind macramé thread from a small ball tightly between them in all directions. If a saw cut is made on each corner of the frame, the nearest one can be used for holding the loose end at start and finish, although the thread will also be wound several times round some of the nails to keep it taut.

Thin but quite rigid materials may be arranged on this network and might include coloured acetate, curved cane, straws, or curly shavings threaded through it, with copper and aluminium strip bent round threads to anchor them in place. Contrasting lines may be wound across, using coloured wool or lurex from ball and spool. Various effects may be tried and alterations made but when a coloured background to the work is desired it must be provided at the start by pinning paper inside the box.

Polystyrene and cocktail sticks

A child may learn to extend his use of the space around him if he is given material that he can place in all directions. Let him experiment with polystyrene shapes broken from sheets of polystyrene or blocks cut with a saw from the thick walls and shaped sections of larger polystyrene containers. Effective colour contrasts may be obtained by painting some of the polystyrene with cellulose filler and then two coats of powder tempera colour before cutting. The pieces can be joined very easily by pushing wooden cocktail sticks into each surface.

Sometimes a pupil who might appear to possess reasonable hand movement has weak and insensitive fingers which hamper his performance. They are often strengthened through creative activities such as making mosaics where results can only be obtained if a little pressure is exerted while making the finger movements. Such exercise will help to strengthen the fingers and stimulate a defective sense of touch.

Cotton net

Mosaic can be created on a background where coarse cotton vegetable net has been laid and PVA (polymer medium) spread over the top to stick it in position. The gauge of the mesh will then help to guide a pupil in placing small units within it. More PVA should be spread over a small area at a time so that the units will be glued in position.

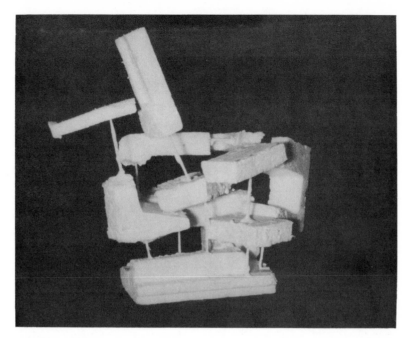

Construction in polystyrene. Age 12 years. Cerebral palsy, athetosis. Special school

Mosaic on cotton net. Age 12 years. E.S.N. Special school

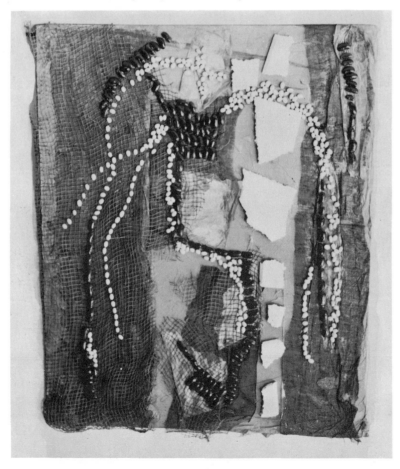

Plasticine

Plasticine that has been rolled out with a rolling-pin, provides a suitable surface on which to practise the placing of mosaic. First attempts might include the making of a 'jewel' on plasticine which has been pressed inside a small polystyrene food container. If it is started by placing the main central shape, such as a large button, the arranging of all subsequent pieces may be guided by this, while the limitations imposed through using the shaped container will help pupils to place them.

Plasticine provides a sensitive surface for an indented design which can be made by pressing a whole variety of different objects into it and lifting them off again.

A sample tile can be made by smoothing the plasticine into a flat shape with the finger-tips. Place a thin strip of wood each side of the plasticine and roll it with a rolling-pin so as to produce

Tile. Age 16 years. Cerebral palsy, hemiplegic. Special school

an even thickness. Use a wood, perspex or card template as a guide for cutting the tile.

Shapes and textures will be made on the surface with those materials which a pupil is able to handle. Besides working with objects of the bolder plastic bottle and spool variety, he should be encouraged to try impressing smaller ones such as corks, buttons or the heads of large nails.

It is possible to take a cast of the impressed design by building up a wall of plasticine round the 'tile' and pouring a mixture of plaster of Paris or Polyfilla (Spackle) inside. When this has set really hard, all plasticine may be peeled away to leave a tile or plaque that can be coloured with shoe polish or paint.

Mosaic in plasticine.
Age 9 years. E.S.N.
Special school

Polyfilla (Spackle) and grated newspaper

If a bolder and more direct method is needed for impressing shapes, try a fairly stiff mixture of Polyfilla and newspaper which has been rubbed into fragments over a wire mesh cheese grater. This mixture will remain in workable condition for approximately three-quarters of an hour, which allows for trial efforts to be made, yet it has the added advantage of drying out quickly afterwards.

Spreading this evenly over a one foot square polystyrene tile, will provide excellent exercise in the use of flat hand movements, as the desired surface can only be obtained by means of a polishing motion with all the fingers fully extended. After

Impressions on Polyfilla (Spackle) and grated newspaper. Age 13 years. E.S.N. Special school

objects have been pressed into the mixture and removed, small finger movements are needed to smooth inside the impressions.

Clay and plaster

A plaster mould can be made of shapes which have been impressed on clay.

Shapes should be impressed on white clay that has been rolled out on a modelling board with a rolling-pin. The edges should be trimmed and a clay wall built round them so that dental plaster or plaster of Paris can be poured inside and left to set hard. Everything, including the modelling board, should then be held under running water until the clay becomes moist enough for the walls and plaster mould to be eased away. The mould should then be washed and cleaned with a sponge or soft brush.

Metal

Nails can be hammered through tin lids so as to make patterns with the holes. The lids may then be sewn on cloth or attached to structures (see page 110).

Metal foil can also be impressed by hammering various metal shapes onto it to make interesting surface textures.

Plaster mould from impressed clay. Age 13 years. Secondary modern school, lowest stream

Impressed metal foil. Age 13 years. Violent epileptic. Special school

Colour magazines

Paper tearing will provide exercise for strengthening the flexibility of the fingers. Tone value in colour can also be learned by many backward and E.S.N. pupils when they arrange shapes torn with the fingers from coloured magazine illustrations or advertisements.

Torn shapes should be sorted immediately into heaps of red, blue, green or yellow. Red may include crimson, scarlet, orange, pink or purple reds, and each of the other piles will contain an equally wide range. Colour magazines can often provide the more subtle tones of colour which a pupil has not yet learned to mix for himself. The shapes from one pile should then be pasted solidly over a sheet of paper, when visually exciting results will depend upon making contrasts between the dark, light and medium tones.

Rug and embroidery needle

There is great value in any simple skill which enables handicapped children to associate the repetition of movement with creativity.

This needle threaded with wool or yarn still attached to the ball can be used both for working outlines and for filling in spaces. It is possible to create embroideries or small hard-wearing mats when two simple movements have been mastered. These consist of pushing the needle to its limit into fabric stretched over a frame and withdrawing the point just sufficiently for this to be repeated. Linen, crash (coarse linen) or hessian (sacking) may be used and no wastage of materials is involved, since attempts are rapidly pulled out and only desired effects need be left permanently.

When an easy rhythm has been established, crinkly yarn may be used in the needle to give line variation and texture. Line contrasts will also be made by sometimes working two or three rows closely together and in inventing deviations. A child may be guided in making outlines by following the shape of his work

Needle for use with continuous ball of thread

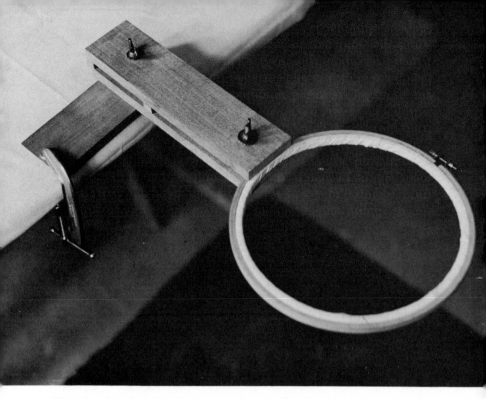

Three lengths of wood with two winged nuts and bolts are needed to make this simple press which will hold an embroidery frame. It is fixed to the table edge with a small G clamp (C cramp). Embroidery and mat making can thus be made possible for many spastics who can use only one hand

Section of a mat. Age 13 years. Cerebral palsy, hemiplegic. Special school

Age 11 years. Cerebral palsy, hemiplegic, severely handicapped, with the use of only two fingers. Special school. Embroidery worked with white weaving yarn that has an alternating thick and thin thread

frame or by working outside or within the rigid rims of boxes staked in place with long hairpins pushed through the taut fabric. One simple polystyrene print can be given tactile qualities by working parts of it in close texture and adding lines.

Cords, strings and strips

Shapes of interesting texture can be created by using a large-eyed sewing needle to couch continuous lengths of different materials on to a strong fabric background that has been stretched over a wooden frame.

Materials suitable for this purpose are: cords or packaging strings, ranging from white through tones of cream, fawn and brown; polypropylene twine in white and brilliant colours; natural and synthetic basket canes; wires of various gauges; thick rug wool and lurex knitting yarn; strips of fabric, both patterned and plain; strips of polythene about half an inch wide, cut to shape with a sharp craft knife used against a metal ruler.

It is often helpful if work can be evolved round a basic shape, such as an aluminium lid which has had holes punched in it so that it can be sewn in position.

Couching. Age 16 years. E.S.N. Special school

Shapes and spaces

When some pupils place their materials, they may gradually learn to attach importance to making a satisfactory arrangement with the shapes and will later apply this knowledge in other forms of creativity. All too often many may fail to express themselves adequately in drawing, painting or collage, where they are required to correlate several ideas, because they can only conceive them as separate parts. In activities where there is opportunity actually to handle three-dimensional form, these pupils may realize the arrangement of their materials in a more tangible way.

Each background should be of a firm material such as fibreboard, plywood or sheets of expanded polystyrene. These materials have thickness which the children can feel. They may then be taught to recognize the background as a shape too, a shape that demands as much of their attention as those which are placed upon its surface. Many pupils will be helped in relating their creation to this background shape if they learn to regard spaces and shapes as being of equal importance.

Therefore when shapes are not needed in proximity, as for mosaic, a satisfactory arrangement of units can be made by watching or feeling the spaces left between each shape. Arrangements are uninteresting where spacing is even and the all too usual scattered appearance could be avoided simply by varying the space between each shape. This will also include distances from edges of the background which is the dominant shape.

It is essential that methods and materials selected will allow for considerable experiment before shapes are finally fixed in position.

String and wire

Some backward and E.S.N. pupils can be made aware of space shapes by creating vertical structures in string and wire.

A picture frame with small brass nails evenly spaced all round will make a useful piece of apparatus on which vertical structures in string or fine to medium gauge wire can be created. It should be wound in two or more directions, and a variety of material can be added to it, either by threading it on or attaching it with florist's wire.

String structures can afterwards be removed, threaded onto wooden dowel rods and hung up. Where wire has been used, a structure may either be suspended from above or made free standing by attaching it with staples to a wooden base.

Hanging structure. Age 14 years. E.S.N. Special school

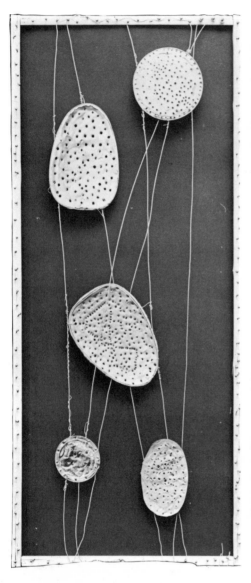 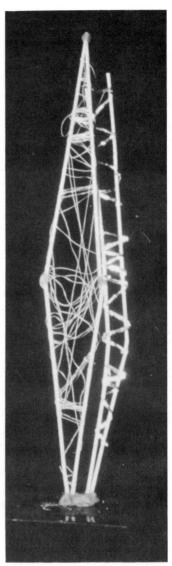

(left) Tin lids on wire. Two boys age 12 years. Secondary modern school, lowest stream

(right) Construction of drinking straws, plasticine, cotton and metal foil. Age 14 years. E.S.N. Special school

Canes

Hanging structures can be made by wiring two canes together at the middle to form a cross and attaching light materials such as corks and milk bottle tops. It is possible to create really large pieces of work in this way.

Wire

It is important that activities should help a child to realize fully the basic quality of the material that he uses. Wire, for instance, could be cut into lengths and joined together to make a framework which might be completed by covering it with paper strips. This, however, does not draw attention to the resilient properties of wire. It is of more value to the E.S.N. pupil or slow learner to create shape by coiling his wire. It is possible to make a complete construction in this way by using different gauges, including fine florist's wire.

Wire that is wound into a solid flat coil of approximately two inches in diameter and then coiled upwards about its circumference to form a tube may be gently pulled out to form the head and body of some fantastic creature. Smaller evenly spaced coils can be made by winding wire firmly round the entire length of a pencil, which should be rotated so that the

Coiled wire. Age 11 years. Secondary modern school, lowest stream

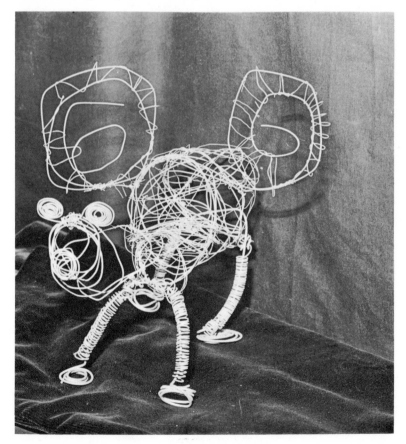

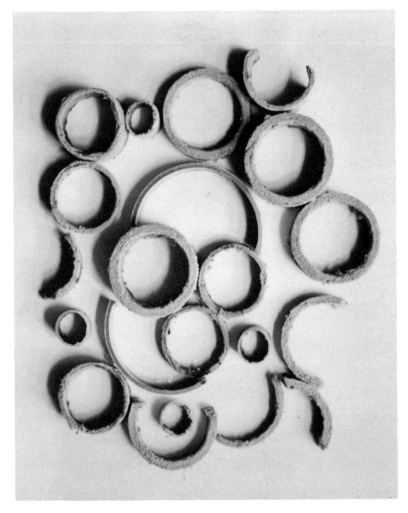

Cardboard curves. Age 12 years. Secondary modern school, lowest stream

top of thumb and forefinger are involved in movements like those required to wind a watch. A strong hand and wrist movement will be needed to rotate and pull the pencil to remove it from the coil. Fine wire is most suitable for joining shapes.

It is important that pupils should fashion their wire directly from the original coil. Not only is this method safer, since there will be no loose uncontrolled end, but also if lengths are cut after the required amount has been used, there is less likelihood of ideas being curtailed through insufficient material. Much frustration from making false starts will thus be avoided, while the tendency to make unnecessary joins and niggling shape is minimized.

The variation from strong to small movements which are involved makes this activity particularly suitable for those with spina bifida, and the physical energy required will make it a suitable activity for some who display an aggressive mood.

Cardboard tubes

Cardboard postal tubes are ideal for making three-dimensional constructions. They may be cut into slices or in half down the middle with a tenon saw. All edges should be smoothed with fine sandpaper before the sections are arranged on a large sheet of cardboard and glued in position.

Printing

A physically handicapped child will often lack the experience of rhythm that is associated with easy natural movement and such play activities as skipping or bouncing balls. This will be particularly the case where there has been any brain damage, of which those with cerebral palsy are but one example. There will be many others who, although they may appear physically normal, show poor mental and physical co-ordination because of brain damage. An E.S.N. boy, for example, who was handicapped in this way, could always be seen to run clumsily about the games field in the opposite direction from the ball that he was trying hard to reach.

There are others who, after the removal of a brain tumour, may have to relearn skills that they had already acquired, such as reading and writing, besides re-establishing some rhythmic movement in a now limp hand or arm. Accident victims too, recently recovered from a fractured skull, may find their manual dexterity impaired, particularly in the finer movements. All these pupils may therefore be helped by methods which will involve the development of movement rhythms.

Two basic needs must be fulfilled if this is to be achieved effectively through the printing of pattern. First, the unit selected for printing must be such that it will adjust easily to any hand and finger movement available, the more rigid materials being unsuitable for this particular purpose. Secondly, the means for recharging a unit with colour should not detract the pupil from his repetitive placing of it, but be so quick that it becomes part of one continuous process. It is then possible by practice to develop individual movement rhythms.

Since success in spacing the pattern unit evenly is primarily dependent upon maintaining a steady rhythm of movement, visual judgement will be of less importance than realizing the physical sensation which this involves. Rhythm printing is suitable for those with cerebral palsy who, apart from unco-ordinated movement, may also have an additional handicap of erratic vision.

Where handicapped children already possess a good sense of rhythm, it can be used to widen the scope of their creative activities. The partially sighted, for instance, who often reveal a rhythmic sense in their singing and other musical activity, may be helped in placing their material by working to music, for it is through using rhythm in pattern making that they may even work on a scale which extends beyond their focal range.

Many young mongol pupils seem to be no different from the normal child in enjoying the sensation of movement, shown in the way in which they will push small model cars to and

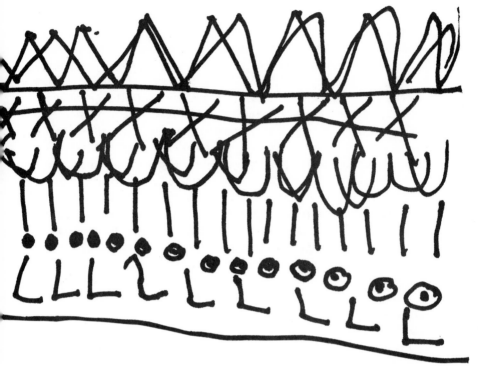

Free pattern drawn with felt pen. Age 15 years. Down's syndrome (mongolism). S.S.N. Junior training centre

fro on the floor. This play activity may be developed as an introduction to pattern making if they are encouraged to run the wheels across foam pads that have been saturated with paint and then push them over sheets of newspaper spread about the floor. Many have a good sense of rhythm and will readily take to rhythmic printing. One fifteen-year-old girl who had learned to read and write would also use letter forms to create rows of pattern.

It is sometimes noticeable that where emotional instability can cause a child's work and behaviour to be so variable that he can experience no steady routine in life, this may also show an inability to appreciate or produce a simple repetitive arrangement of pattern.

In cases of muscular dystrophy the muscle weakens and becomes progressively worse as time goes on, until the pupil has difficulty in manipulating the heavier objects or exercising much downward pressure. It is important that he should be helped to join in creative activity for as long as possible, if only for the purpose of directing his attention from this diminishing ability. His morale can be maintained by giving him the lightest possible printing units and introducing other interesting methods of printing. At the same time, a child who has brittle bones and fingers can be so frustrated by lack of activity that he may become difficult in his behaviour. Again, careful selection of printing units will enable him to take part and, in this case, strengthen his movements through gradual use.

Rhythmic movements of the arm to and fro when printing make this a suitable activity for those with physical and mental handicaps of a totally different nature, when it may either help to develop a rhythm sense or stimulate one that already exists. The experimental nature of printing activities in a class where there are pupils with mixed handicaps will enable each member to work within a range of materials which he can manage most successfully. A pupil who uses the simplest of these or is only able to exert minimal physical effort, can still make a valuable contribution in the class with the effects he has obtained from his particular printing units. The interest which this will arouse should help many to dwell less upon the extent of their own handicaps.

Fabrics with boldly woven or printed checks and stripes may sometimes be introduced instead of paper to guide the placing of units, but these do not help pupils who are only able to appreciate boundaries which they can feel. The ability to print a regular arrangement of shapes may be acquired when the movements of pressing the unit from pad to paper have become rhythmic through much practice. While such rhythm can be maintained the spacing will actually improve and its creator be made physically aware of pattern.

The number of pattern rows which can be printed with any success is largely determined by the distance which the pupil can reach comfortably from one working position. When it becomes necessary to adjust this or the surface that is being printed, that particular work rhythm will be broken and any new one cause the spacing to differ.

It is therefore hardly surprising that many wheel-chair cases will manage little more than two rows of a pattern at each attempt, while others can decorate short lengths of wrapping paper or fabric, and will be able to print borders or place mats and narrower widths of pattern which are later joined together with machine stitching to make an effective hanging.

When selecting suitable printing units it is advisable to concentrate on light, flexible materials, as these can often be gripped between fingers which have a very limited action. They will adjust immediately to every hand movement, so it will also be possible for a child to feel indirectly any contact that is made through them.

Rubber leaf turner

Although a child with cerebral palsy may have only a couple of useful fingers, printing might still be attempted with a rubber leaf turner, readily available from stationers, worn like a thimble on one or both fingers. Make sure that it fits the child tightly, as only then will he be able to use his maximum finger pressure for printing the top or side of this rubber surface.

Sponge

Many handicapped children will find the use of a sponge a good introduction to printing, and when their interest has been aroused they will often show great determination in finding a way to print other materials.

Household objects

Pliable plastic bottles usually print shapes in outline only, but if the base is cut out and some rolled foam rubber inserted, an interesting texture can be produced. A loofah, ball of string, or bobbly wool may also be tried, while even the slight resilience of a pine cone enables some pupils to hold it and feel its top touch the surface of the paper as they print.

It is by being introduced to a variety of commonplace materials for printing that many physically and mentally handicapped pupils may begin to appreciate the nature of things around them, as through manipulating these for a specific purpose they can acquire some knowledge concerning size, shape and texture.

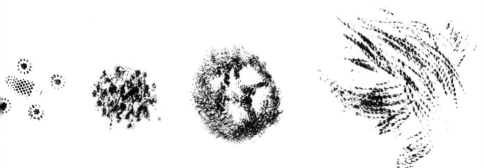

Prints from a rubber leaf turner, ball of bobbly wool, a loofah and a ball of string

Prints from a pine cone

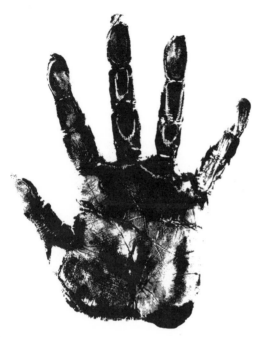

Age 12 years. Emotionally disturbed. Secondary modern school. Printing the hand can be an incentive for some spastics to use it in a flat position. It also provides the mentally handicapped with a tangible printing unit which they may arrange in different ways

Prints from rolled foam rubber

Spring whisk

A pupil who is able to use only two or three fingers for gripping his material will often manage those units best which have thin handles made of wire, such as the simple culinary spring whisk. In acquiring the light touch which will depress this fully in one dramatic movement, he may then realize, despite his lack of manual strength, that some downward pressure is needed for printing.

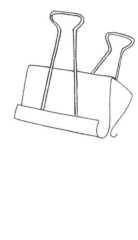

A spring whisk and a spring clip

Spring clip

Objects with an interesting shape or texture suitable for printing but too small to hold, may be used if they are fixed inside a spring or bulldog clip.

Prints from a spring whisk and a bicycle pedal block

Nylon pot scourer

The nylon pot scourer gives a feeble print, but if each time it is pressed on the printing surface the hand can be rotated to left or right, some indication of this movement is actually printed. Encouragement to achieve this bolder effect could help to develop the flexibility of a wrist.

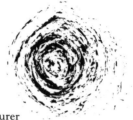

Print from a nylon pot scourer

Glass bottles

Those with cerebral palsy who display too fierce a grip will often be able to print with heavier, rigid glass bottles. But it is by giving these pupils light materials for printing and the bottles to others with a poor grip that both may learn to adjust their movements through practising control of their respective materials.

Printing with glass bottles. Age 12 years. Cerebral palsy, ataxia. Special school

Polystyrene

A physically handicapped pupil may sometimes be able to make an interesting surface with which to print.

A piece of polystyrene cut from a container or broken from a ceiling tile may be used for printing. Lines or spots can be made on this soft surface with a six-inch file, which will be more easily controlled if used without a handle so that the fingers come in direct contact with it. The pointed end will also be useful for making spots. A line-cutting tool could be used too. Lines may be made or areas removed by scraping it along with the edge facing downwards.

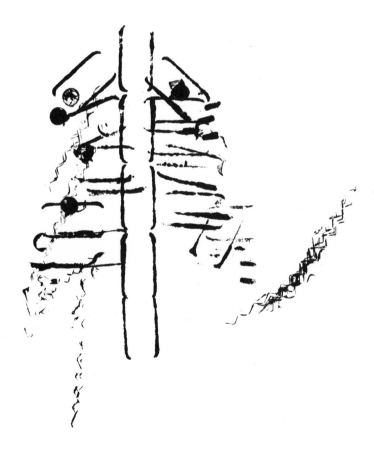

'Decorated Christmas tree'. Age 10 years. Cerebral palsy, quadriplegic. Special school. Both ends of a plastic bottle were printed and a wooden pastry trimmer was rolled across the paper

Printing with polystyrene. Age 11 years. Cerebral palsy, athetosis. Special school

Printing pads

A useful printing pad is made of sheet foam rubber that is cut into a six-inch square. Press it on to a wooden workboard behind two narrow strips of thin aluminium that have been nailed in position about five inches apart. The pad should be on the side of the board nearest the child's useful hand and should leave plenty of room for printing.

One foam pad that has been charged with black or a colour can enable a wheel-chair pupil to enjoy a period of independent practice printing on newsprint, kitchen, or coloured tissue paper. Later, dyed butter muslin can be printed if the foam pad is charged with a fabric dye mixed with water, or fabric ink to which thinning oil has been added.

These pads will keep their resilience if they are stored in plastic bags after use.

Clothes wringer

A pupil in a wheel-chair, unlike one who can stand, is limited in the use of his body weight and will often be unable to exert much downward pressure for printing a large unit. A clothes wringer may well solve the problem.

Fabric for a large single print from polystyrene sheet should be stretched over cardboard for easier handling and fixed at the back with sticking plaster. Ink the polystyrene on foam rubber and lay the fabric over it. Keep it in place with two clothes pegs on each side, which should be positioned a couple of inches from each end. In order for the pegs to be clipped on more easily, lay a book on the fabric to hold it in position and push the polystyrene so that it projects sufficiently over the edge of the table.

Use a small clothes wringer for printing. Let the pupil feed the work into it as the handle is turned for him. Although in cerebral palsy a pupil often has difficulty in releasing his grip quickly, fingers will be safeguarded when the first pegs bring the rollers to a halt. All pegs should then be unclipped and the material can continue through the wringer unguided as the rollers are again set in motion.

Inked rubber roller

Some pupils will be able to experiment in making prints by rolling a six-inch inked rubber roller on paper which has been fixed over a textured surface such as fine wire mesh or tree bark. Many children obviously delight in the almost magical way in which the image appears on the paper.

The value of any activity for handicapped children must, however, always be considered in relation to their individual needs and not simply the pleasure it gives them.

Print made with an inked roller over bark

Crayon rubbings

Other pupils may only appreciate textures when they can feel them. Let them rub a thick crayon over paper that has been secured over a textured surface. They will then feel the vibrations as they rub.

Corrugated cardboard

An E.S.N. child may progress from experiencing textures in the way described above to creating textural effects for himself.

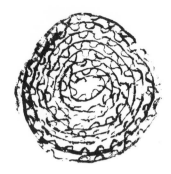

Print made with rolled corrugated cardboard

Corrugated cardboard may be printed flat, or strips of it may be rolled and held in position with an elastic band to produce an entirely different effect.

Paper

Stiff crumpled paper can be used as an introductory unit for rhythm printing and to create areas of texture.

Paper will also produce an interesting print if it is first folded, so that not all parts can come in contact with the ink when this is applied with a rubber roller.

Similar experiments may be carried out by substituting other materials such as tarlatan, surgical gauze or cotton net.

Children at S.S.N. level will learn to print shapes by dropping blobs of coloured paint in the centre of their paper and folding it in half while the paint is still wet. Results are purely chance effects. Creative activity for the E.S.N., on the other hand,

Crumpled paper: a first attempt at printing. Age 10 years. Down's syndrome (mongolism). S.S.N. Junior training centre

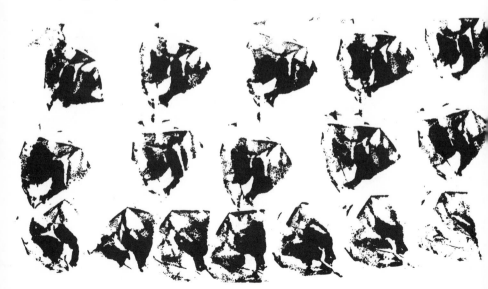

Print made with folded paper

'Symmetry'. Age 12 years. Emotionally disturbed. Secondary modern school, lowest stream

should demand the exercise of some deliberate intention, so that through simple experiment pupils may develop more positive ideas concerning cause and effect.

An exciting symmetrical base shape for a decorative mask can often be obtained if the paper is creased down the middle and fairly thick paint is applied to one half only, so that it prints in reverse when folded over and pressed. Pupils may learn through attempting several of these that further detail might be included by perhaps leaving a space for an eye, or making other modifications at that stage, which they had not foreseen. When the shape is dry, other methods may be used for printing shapes and textures on the surface.

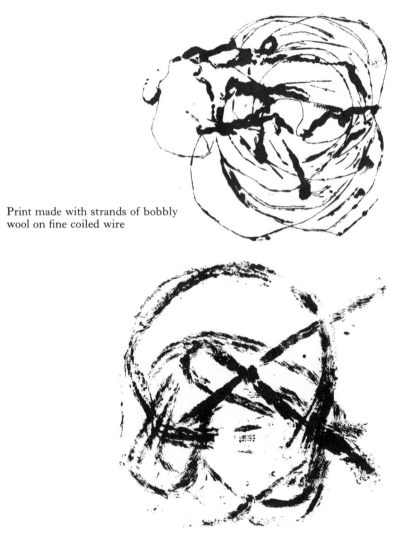

Print made with strands of bobbly wool on fine coiled wire

Print made with knotted plastic 'string'

Threads

Coarse or fine threads can be used for printing and might include plain wool, fancy weaving yarn, string, sewing-cotton and synthetic materials.

Most E.S.N. pupils are noticeably poor at tying serviceable knots and if alternative means of holding threads taut are not introduced, their experience in creating textures with threads will be very limited.

Threads, however, may be wound for printing over a wood base with the ends secured in slits made at appropriate places. Threads may also be used in conjunction with rubber bands or wound about a coil of fine wire which, apart from providing additional material for creating line contrasts, helps to keep them in place.

Rolling-pin

The rolling-pin provides a method of printing which may help a pupil to produce variation in both line and direction.

When threads are attached to a rolling-pin they can be charged with ink by rolling it over an inked pad. It is then possible to obtain different effects without changing the units, depending on whether the rolling-pin is rotated completely, rolled to and fro, or used in several directions.

Wool wound round a rolling-pin and worked to and fro

After practising these techniques many E.S.N. pupils may attempt to create textures and shapes by starting with plain surfaces, although a definite lead must be given which will allow for experiment without ruining the material. When this is not done, we may quite unwittingly add to a child's feeling of inadequacy by presenting him with a material on which he must create directly and where one false move across the pristine surface may spell immediate failure.

Trial efforts are necessary not only for giving the child experience but also because they act as a kind of shock absorber in which such tensions are released that would otherwise

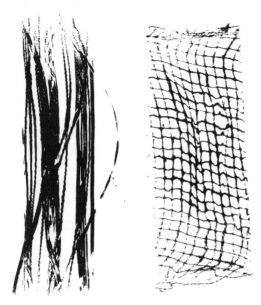

Elastic bands round a rolling-pin that is worked in one direction only, and cotton net on a rolling-pin

impede creativity. This makes it necessary to introduce methods that are still flexible enough to give pupils ample opportunity for adding, discarding, or rearranging any part before producing results. Lino blocks, card and cardboard can all be used in this way.

(left) Pine needles on a lino block

(right) Grasses on a lino block

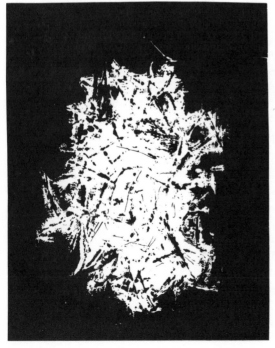

Packing straws

Lino blocks

To ink the block, squeeze or pour a little printing ink on to a piece of glass and work a rubber roller over it in all directions. Then work the roller over the printing surface before placing paper on top and applying even pressure over it with another rubber roller.

A child may experiment with a lino block by dropping threads, pine needles or grasses on to the inked surface before printing with it. Alternatively, shapes made of paper, cotton net or surgical gauze can be used to mask out an area before printing. Another variation would be to overprint, creating three shaded areas in light, medium and dark tones. This will produce interesting colour and textural effects where they overlap.

Cardboard

When several shapes are to be used in one print, pupils should be encouraged deliberately to vary the spacing between each, as this will inevitably lead them to create a more interesting arrangement than one where everything is evenly spaced. Round smooth stones of varying sizes that can be moved about on a surface are often useful for working out such an arrangement.

Simple shapes may be cut on thick cardboard with a knife. The tip of the knife should then be used to lift up areas inside the shapes so that they can easily be peeled away. When a print is taken, 'peeled' areas will remain ink-free.

Impressions can also be made by hammering large nails and chisels of different sizes on the surface, which may be smoothed gently with fine sandpaper. A thin coat of shellac over this will make a non-absorbent surface that is easy to print.

'Stones'. A cardboard print. Age 11 years. Emotionally disturbed. Secondary modern school, lowest stream

Card

Different shapes of the same thickness may be glued to a surface to form a relief that can be printed. Card is ideal for this process.

Use three rectangles of card. They should be of approximately the same height but should vary in width. (Card of six-sheet thickness is best.) Each rectangle should then be divided into two pieces by cutting in a curve from top to bottom. The shapes should then be decorated by cutting into them with a hole punch.

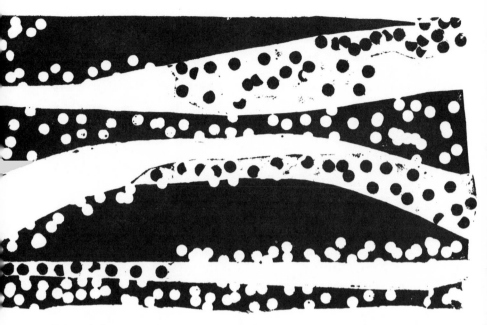

Print of shapes cut from cardboard rectangles, combined with the use of a press punch

Some of the shapes should then be glued on to a sheet of card, including some of the punched-out pieces, which should be added to the spaces in between. When the adhesive has dried the 'block' can be printed.

Puppets

Simple puppets have proved extremely valuable in play therapy, for it is realized that there are occasions when the child will readily identify himself with a puppet and under the guise of its personality work out his own thoughts and actions, even without a curtain to hide behind. Since a childhood neurosis is generally small or recent, it can often be healed through dramatic and imaginative play of this kind, when expressing the emotion in action will ease the moral pressure and so make the repression more bearable.

Puppetry can also be a community activity when the aim is for pupils to entertain others with the puppets which they make. It will then provide valuable opportunities for the handicapped in their learning to be members of a team working to fulfil an objective, yet much of the work will still depend upon individual achievement. There is opportunity on a project of this kind, with activities that include the production of scenery, stage properties, curtains, puppets or programme covers, for each child to become involved according to his ability. Those who may find difficulty either in making or manipulating their own puppet often prove efficient stage managers, curtain operators and controllers of sound effects. When the production begins to take shape, each member of this team, whatever his role, will realize some feeling of personal responsibility in trying to make it a success. He is also now in a position where even his own successful participation depends upon co-operation with others. The crowning sense of achievement comes, however, when these children find themselves able to enthral an audience, for it will be then that their own frustrations will be forgotten and they will experience a deeply satisfying positive self-feeling that is based upon maintaining successful personal relationships.

The kind of performance most suitable for the physically and mentally handicapped is one in which they can concentrate on creating some purposeful movement with their puppet. This presents valuable opportunities for some of the handicapped to practise manipulative therapy and the teacher must decide whether the working of a glove, string or rod puppet can provide a movement pattern that will be most beneficial to the individual pupil. Music becomes an essential part of the plan through which children may learn to synchronize these movements with the rhythm. Since the music will eventually be recorded on tape, they will be able to pick out their cue according to the tune that is being played.

It is quite possible for a well-known fairy tale to be mimed in this way, but variety shows are always popular and rather easier to produce, since each item is complete in itself and those who manipulate the puppets have only to work on one part. It will be found with E.S.N. pupils that if they are asked to resolve one such situation, this is really enough for them to manage satisfactorily, and although many can learn to scatter their performance throughout the sequence of a story, much more rehearsing is needed. A ballet item based upon the antics of animals at the zoo, brass bands and double acts will therefore continue to be produced enthusiastically.

Many E.S.N. pupils are lacking in self-confidence and often it is only made possible for them to project their imagination into the actions of a puppet through the knowledge that they are completely hidden from the view of an audience. As manipulative skill increases, the scope for exercising some initiative becomes greater and it is always interesting to find that through working together children invariably introduce humorous incidents which they have evolved entirely between themselves.

Making puppets

It is possible to make glove, string or rod puppets using the same simple method in which no sewing is required. The head may be modelled boldly with a mixture of finely grated newspaper and cellulose paste to which a little cellulose filler has been added. This can be built up on a cardboard postal tube that has been thickened at one end with strips of pasted newspaper. A longer tube, which will keep the body rigid during the performance, should be used for both string and rod puppets.

Two cloth squares may be used for making a body. They should be glued round the cardboard neck and then stuck together with fabric adhesive across the shoulders and down the sides, leaving armholes approximately two inches wide.

The legs and arms for string puppets can be made from single lengths of rolled buckram. These may be attached to the body with small metal split curtain rings pierced through both cloth and buckram. This will allow for easy movement. Glove puppets will only require lengths of buckram glued inside the armholes, although many pupils also like to add legs. Where loose limbs are used it will be necessary to attach weighted hands and feet. These can be made by pressing sticking plaster over the buckram ends and then round short pieces of lead-weighted curtain tape. If the body fabric is brightly coloured, bold contrasts will be easy to achieve by simply sticking on fringes and braids which also help to hide the rings or untidy edges.

String puppets require two lengths of linen thread or nylon fishing-line attached to the head. They should be tied round

Music and movement with string puppets. Age 15 years. E.S.N. Special school

Rod or hand puppet theatre. Age 10 years. Junior school, lower stream

String puppet theatre. Age 14 years. E.S.N. Special school

String puppets. Age 10 years. Junior school, lower stream

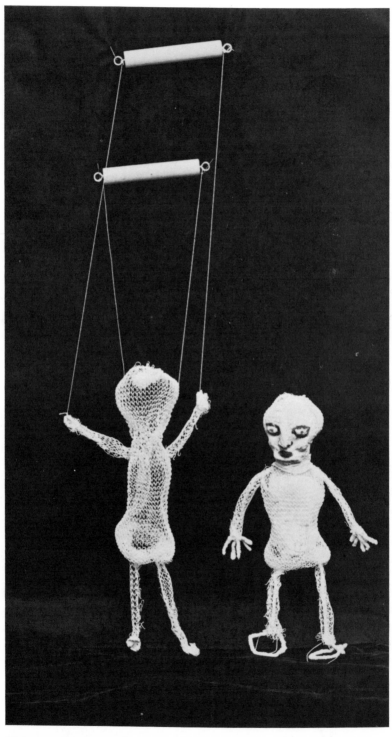

String puppets from nylon pot scourers. Age 13 years. E.S.N. Special school

screw-eyes, one on each side of the head, and then attached to two more eyes on the ends of a short wooden dowel rod control. Two more lengths for controlling limb movements should be fixed in the same way to another short dowel rod to be held in the other hand. The choice of limbs to which these will be attached depends upon the particular movement required of the puppet. Action can be obtained by tilting this second dowel rod in the appropriate direction.

A rod puppet will require only movable arms, which are obtained by attaching a dowel stick to the extremity of each. This puppet is manipulated by holding the long tube with one hand while using the other to move the rods. Slow stately characters that can wear long robes with sleeve drapes to help conceal the rods are the best choice for this kind of puppet.

The glove puppet, as its name implies, should be made to fit the hand. The simplest method of manipulating it is to grip the tube between the palm and the third, fourth, and fifth fingers, while using the thumb and index finger for creating arm movements in the puppet.

Nylon pot scourers

The pot scourer purchased as a rounded pad is usually made from one coarse but resilient nylon net bag which, if pulled from the inside, will present a form that can represent the head, neck and body of a puppet. Legs and arms can then be made from rolled lengths of similar net, such as the plastic net in which fruit is purchased. Attach the limbs to the body with strong stitching or split rings.

String puppets made from pot scourers merely require lead-weighted curtain tape at the end of each limb. The nylon mesh has a gossamer appearance that seems to invite decoration with delicate materials such as lurex threads, beads and sequins. This method of making string puppets is often most suitable where, for instance, several dancers are required on the stage at one time. It is then that the combination of simple form and its decoration can prove more important in creating the fantasy than a striving for the bolder features that are required by a main character.

Animals or insect puppets can also be made from nylon pot scourers. Both head and body shape may be stuffed with tissue paper, although this may sometimes be done only as a temporary measure to make it easier to sew on fabric or beads or to model the face. The face can be made with torn pieces of tissue paper

A scene from 'Cinderella' mimed to music with string puppets. Age 15 years.
E.S.N. Special school

that are modelled with the fingers on to the mesh surface that
has first been coated with PVA adhesive.

Models for dressing in period costume can be made by
omitting the weights and sewing the arms and legs over pipe-
cleaners. An arc of medium-gauge galvanized iron wire is then
placed inside the body so that the ends can be threaded through
each leg and fashioned into flat loops which enable the figure
to stand.

Conclusions

There is a common factor throughout art teaching with both physically and mentally handicapped pupils that rests in a teacher's capacity to simplify the learning situation for each individual child. He must be able to assess the pupil's mental and physical capabilities, provide a suitable range of activities and experiences for him and be able to sense the exact moment at which to introduce a new activity, to offer help, or give encouragement. How the handicapped come to regard themselves will very much depend upon the attitude of mind which they develop as a result of these experiences, for the success of their personal or social adjustment may be greatly influenced by such achievements. It is essential, therefore, that the handicapped should realize some measure of personal success for it will be upon this foundation that further and often all-round progress can be made. These results, however, do not materialize quickly; the rate of improvement may be almost imperceptible in some, taking years rather than weeks or months to achieve.

Art has an important role in both the diagnostic and therapeutic field since we are concerned not only with the child as a learner but also in his development as a person. Our first practical consideration may be to choose activities for their therapeutic value, that can help to improve sensory, spatial or visuo-motor ability and co-ordination in general. Art education can also be so directed that it provides channels by which many handicapped children are helped in organizing their own environment into meaningful stimuli. They may then not only realize themselves and also their relationship to their surroundings more fully, but also develop some simple concepts necessary for more formal teaching or purposeful activity.

Creative activity can help the blind or deaf in overcoming their detachment from the environment and by this means we can also help others, who in extreme cases may not altogether experience themselves as a psychic entity apart from the world around them. In others it will become the means for building up confidence through newly acquired ability which might even become the basis for leisure interests that will help to maintain their mental health in the years ahead. This could prove invaluable, too, for those who cannot make use of language to communicate with others, by giving them an alternative means of expressing themselves. Since such activity provides the opportunity for self-expression and also a vital release of emotional energy in some positive form, it will play an important role in the rehabilitation of those who are emotionally disturbed or maladjusted.

When, therefore, creative activity can be used to encourage

the fullest development of the reduced potentialities in those who are handicapped, it becomes a fundamental part of their education through which they are able to experience not only a fuller physical awareness but also a mental awakening.

Bibliography

Born that way by Earl R. Carlson. John Day, New York. 1941.
A. James, Worcs. 1953

The Special Child by Barbara Furneaux. Penguin Education
Special. Penguin Books, England. 1969

Handicapped Children by John D. Kershaw. Heinemann
Medical Books, London. 1966

What is Special Education? The proceedings of the First Inter-
national Conference of the Association for Special Education.
Published by the Association for Special Education Ltd,
Stanmore, Middx, England. 1966

Perceptual and Visuo-motor Disorders in Cerebral Palsy by
M. L. J. Abercrombie. Heinemann Medical Books, London.
1964. Lippincott, New York. 1971

Practical Training for the Severely Handicapped Child by Milan
Morgenstern and Helen Löw-Beer. Published by the Spastics
Society Medical Education and Information Unit with
William Heinemann Medical Books, London. 1966

Aspects of Autism, Some Approaches to Childhood Psychoses,
ed. by P. J. Mittler. British Psychological Society, London.
1968

Learning Disabilities, Educational Principles and Practices by
Doris J. Johnson and Helmer R. Myklebust. Grune and
Stratton, New York. Heinemann Medical Books, London.
1967

Special Education. The official journal of the Association for
Special Education and Educational Journal of the Spastics
Society, London.

Art for Spastics by Zaidee Lindsay. Mills and Boon, London.
Taplinger, New York. 1966

Art is for All by Zaidee Lindsay. Mills and Boon, London.
Taplinger, New York. 1967

Learning about Shape by Zaidee Lindsay. Mills and Boon,
London. Taplinger, New York. 1969

Materials and suppliers

A wide range of art and craft materials is available from:
Dryad Ltd, Northgates, Leicester
Water-based block printing colours, fabric dyes, Redimix
Temperacolour, brass rubbing sticks, sheets of metal foil
manufactured by:
Reeves and Sons Ltd, Enfield, Middx.
Available from most shops selling artists' materials.

Waterproof fabric ink and thinning oil:
    T. N. Lawrence & Son, 2-4 Bleeding Heart Yard,
    Greville Street, London EC1
Rug and embroidery needle:
    Arnold Clarke, 69 Falstaff Road, Shirley, Solihull, Warwicks.
Handweaving yarns:
    Hugh Griffiths, 'Brookdale', Beckington, Bath, Somerset

Acknowledgments

I should like to thank W. L. Thomas, B.A., Chief Education Officer, Reading, Berks. for granting me permission to use the photographs of my pupils' work at the Avenue Special School. My thanks also to E. S. Cornell, M.S.c., Headmaster of the Alfred Sutton Secondary Boys' School, Reading, for permission to use the prints and photographs of work produced by my classes.

I am grateful to those who made me welcome within their particular field of special education and for allowing certain illustrations to be reproduced in this book:

Dr A. Gatherer, Medical Officer of Health, Reading

Mrs A. E. Watkins, Head Teacher, Wakefield Lodge Junior Training Centre, Reading (Special School, 1971)

The Chief Nursing Officer, Borocourt Hospital, Wyfold, Reading

A. A. Chappell, Headmaster, Smith Hospital, Henley-on-Thames, Oxon.

Mrs E. Dolton, Principal, and Miss Sheila Osborn, Headmistress, Barclay School for Partially Sighted Girls, Sunninghill, Berks.

P. B. Green, Headmaster, R.N.I.D. Larchmoor School for Maladjusted Deaf Children, Stoke Poges, Bucks.

The Royal National Institute for the Blind, 224 Great Portland Street, London W1, for relevant information.

Remembering, too, all the pupils whose work appears in this book, with particular admiration for those who showed such determination in overcoming severe handicap, that they might be creative.

Index